Praise and Worship

Praise and Worship

by
Rod Parsley

with
Clint Brown

Harrison House
Tulsa, Oklahoma

2nd Printing
Over 12,000 in Print

Praise and Worship
ISBN 0–89274–637-8
Copyright © 1993 by Rod Parsley
World Harvest Church
P. O. Box 32932
Columbus, Ohio 43232

Published by Harrison House, Inc.
P. O. Box 35035
Tulsa, Oklahoma 74153

Praise ye the Lord. Praise ye the Lord from
the heavens: praise him in the heights.
Praise ye him, all his angels: praise ye him,
all his hosts.
Praise ye him, sun and moon: praise him, all
ye stars of light.
Praise him, ye heavens of heavens, and ye
waters that be above the heavens.
Let them praise the name of the Lord: for he
commanded, and they were created,
He hath also established them for ever and
ever: he hath made a decree which shall
not pass.
Praise the Lord from the earth, ye dragons,
and all deeps:
Fire, and hail; snow, and vapours; stormy wind
fulfilling his word:
Mountains, and all hills; fruitful trees, and all
cedars:
Beasts, and all cattle; creeping things, and
flying fowl:
Kings of the earth, and all people; princes, and
all judges of the earth:
Both young men, and maidens; old men, and
children:
Let them praise the name of the Lord: for his
name alone is excellent; his glory is above
the earth and heaven.
He also exalteth the horn of his people, the
praise of all his saints; even of the children
of Israel, a people near unto him. Praise
ye the Lord.

Psalm 148:1–14

Contents

Preface

Praise is not only singing, clapping our hands, or dancing before the Lord, but a lifestyle of thanksgiving to God. Praise builds faith, faith creates miracles, and miracles glorify God.

Praise and worship are more than preliminaries to preaching. They are more than a program; they are more than a ritual. God never intended our praise and worship to be watered down with the religious traditions of man.

We can get so caught up in playing church that we forget we are on a battlefield. On that battlefield of life, our praise —the words we speak — will determine our victory or defeat. Bondages are torn asunder in the presence of heartfelt and unpretentious praise and worship.

We want to place this book in your hands as a tool to help you enter into a realm of praise and worship you have never experienced before. It is our prayer that you will come to know God personally and intimately, and that it will make a difference in your life and the lives of everyone around you.

Allow us to impart a vision of praise and worship into your heart that we might go forth together, glorifying God and establishing His kingdom on the earth.

Rod Parsley, Pastor
Clint Brown, Music Director

Introduction

The young man cowered in the corner of the jail cell. His last memories on the face of the earth were destined to be of this cold, musty cell block. His execution was scheduled for today.

He sat silently, his hands locked around his knees. He heard the jingle of keys and the slow, steady rhythm of the jailer's footsteps in the hallway.

He pressed back against the corner of the cell, feeling the icy tentacles of fear and despair. His heart pounded out a fast, unsteady beat. Could they be coming for him?

The jailer reached his cell. The young man searched the jailer's face for some clue of what was happening. As the key grated in the lock, it reminded him of the bars that held him in — bars of guilt and shame. He knew he was guilty; he was a thief and a murderer.

He had killed a man, and he deserved to die.

The jailer's voice cut through his thoughts. "Get up! You are free to go."

What was he hearing? Could it be true?

The jailer's voice came again, "You are free to go."

Could he believe it?

Slowly, he staggered to his feet. He stepped cautiously past the jailer, fully expecting to be thrown back into the cell.

The young man's pace quickened with each step down the hallway. He looked back only once to see if the jailer was in pursuit.

But the jailer still stood by the empty cell. No one followed; no one stopped him. He was free to go — but why?

As he left the jail, he found the streets packed with people. He now had an idea why he had been released . . . and he knew how he could find out.

As he set out from the jail on his mission, an old friend rushed up to him.

"Hey, man! We heard you were set free," he said. "All of the guys want to celebrate with you at our old hangout. Come on. Let's go!"

The young man shook off the invitation

"No," he replied, "I have someplace I need to go."

He pressed on through the crowd.

Suddenly, he heard the familiar voice of his little sister cutting through the rumble of the crowd.

"Mom and Dad sent me to find you," she yelled. "They have a great party planned! When we found out they were setting you free, we wanted to celebrate."

But not even the desire to see his family could come before what he had to do.

"No," he told her. "I can't come. I have someplace I need to go." He pushed on.

Finally, he made it to the center of the crowd. He tried to force his way through to the front, but his efforts were thwarted by the mass of onlookers. He could get no closer.

He was startled by a voice and a tap on the shoulder.

"Hey, aren't you Barabbas? What are you doing out of jail?" He glanced back to see who spoke to him. "Yes," he replied. "I am Barabbas. I was supposed to die today. I just wanted to see the man who took my place."

Barabbas knew that every so often the governor would release a prisoner in a political move to gain the people's favor. He realized now that he was the prisoner who had been released.

Jesus of Nazareth was the man who had taken his place.

Jesus took our place on the cross. He suffered and He died — instead of us. He paid the price that we might be able to know God.

Do you want to know Him? Do you want your heart to overflow with worship for the One who took your place?

I believe the understanding of praise and worship you will gain from these pages will thrust you into a new dimension of your walk with God. In a new and fresh way, you will begin to understand . . . praise, the ultimate experience, and worship, the ultimate relationship.

1

Understanding Praise and Worship

God is moving in a new way in praise and worship in the body of Christ today. We no longer have to partake of yesterday's leftovers, but we have a fresh move — fresh manna — from the throne room of God. The church is ready for revival: no more six foot icicles moaning and groaning and messing about in the pulpit; no more singing yesterday's songs about tomorrow's blessings.

Music and ministry are one. The return of inspirational preaching and the phenomenal flow of revelation in the church today are spilling over into the realm of praise and worship.

The move of God today is characterized by the supernatural — by the tangible, manifested presence of God; by an outpouring of the gifts of the Spirit; and by altars overflowing with new converts. And the doorway into the supernatural is praise and worship.

Revival is springing to life and sweeping across the country. No man started it, and no man can stop it!

All the major moves of God in the past have given birth to their own music. Many of the great hymns of the church sprang from the Protestant Reformation. The Healing Revival of the 1940s and 1950s had its own music — shaped notes and simple lyrics. Folk style music accompanied by guitar and tambourine came with the Charismatic Renewal. Scripture choruses abounded with the Word of Faith movement.

The move of God today incorporates the best of all that has gone before. Sprinklings of the old help to birth the new. Let's not stop anywhere along the way! Let's take everything God has for us, and go on.

There is a different spirit in praise today. It is fervent, zealous — energized by the strong convictions of a people who know that they know their God. It is forceful . . . it is striking . . . it is irresistible.

There is a different spirit in worship today. It is strong and powerful. It is spontaneous. It is prophetic. It is seasoned by holiness. It reflects the hearts of a people who are living right — who are not in bed with their boyfriend on Saturday night and in church on Sunday morning with their gospel mask on.

We are pulling down the sin barriers and going right into the throne room of God!

Set in the Church

This move of God is seated in the local church. There is an outpouring of souls flooding our altars as they see us praising and worshiping a God we really know. These new believers need a spiritual home where they can be raised up in the nurture and admonition of the Lord.

An understanding of praise and worship is absolutely essential if we are to take our place in the New Testament church.

God spoke to one of my staff ministers the first time he ever set foot in this church.

"If you want to be a part of what I'm doing in these last days," God told him, "you're going to have to be a part of a local church."

He was not tied into a local church at that time, but he made the decision to obey God. He brought his wife and family here, and they made World Harvest Church their church. It's been ten years now, and they have been here ever since.

They both work on my staff, they have both been involved in praise and worship on our platform, and their children are all honor students in our Christian academy. They allowed God to set them in the church, and He has blessed their lives tremendously and used them to bless many others.

Isn't that a better picture than a churchless family just drifting along spiritually in a home that is not a home — with parents getting divorced, rock music blaring, children on crack, bodies filled with disease, and finances in ruin?

I guarantee you this family has seen some problems in the ten years they have been here. But there is no such thing as a perfect church. A church is made up of people, and people still wear earth suits. But this family made a decision that this was their church.

What are we trading for the presence of God in our lives? Do we really have a right to go our own way and do our own thing? It is time to grow up and lay aside our childish ways. Can we put up with a few flaws of human inconsistency to get the blessing of God in our lives? What is it worth to us?

There is no such thing as a perfect church, but there is a church that is perfect for you. Find it, get in it, and stay put.

Choose Life

Praise is the greatest weapon at our disposal. It is a two–edged sword on the lips of the army of God. Proverbs 18:21 says, **"Death and life are in the power of the tongue."** When we choose praise, we choose life. Praise brings life. Complaining leads to compromise, compromise leads to corruption, corruption leads to collapse.

Praise, on the other hand, builds faith, faith creates miracles, and miracles glorify God. If we want to find out what "blesses the Lord," then we're going to have to learn how to praise God. It's not just clapping our hands, and dancing, and singing. It is the faith–filled words of praise that we speak. It is what we say that blesses the Lord.

Our praise blesses the Lord because our attention and our focus are directed toward Him.

Hebrews 11:1 says, **"Now faith is the substance of things hoped for, the evidence of things not seen."** If the word **"faith"** is replaced with the word "praise," it would read like this: **"Now [praise] is the substance of things hoped for, the evidence of things not seen."**

Praise will take us from where we are to where we want to be. Praise looks with the eye of faith, beyond the present circumstances to the desired end.

Sometimes people don't understand that. They tend to think of praise and worship only in terms of music: "I really enjoyed the praise and worship service at church today."

What about praise and worship at home? What about praise and worship on the job? What about that? Praise and worship are often expressed by music, but are certainly not limited to it.

So many times churches get wrapped up in the world's understanding of praise and worship. Fast music is considered praise. Slow music is considered worship. But praise and worship are not based on a tempo or a beat: they are based on the words we are saying.

A song like "Our God Is Able" is praise because it is horizontal — going from person to person. It speaks about the works of God: what He has done, what He is doing, and what He will do — from a basis of fellowship with Him and with each other.

Our God Is Able

Our God is able
Our God is able
Let the heavens sing
Let the saints proclaim
Our God is able.

Our God is able
Our God is able
Satan's standing his ground
But his kingdom's coming down
For our God is able

We won't bend, we won't bow
We're coming out of the fire
With a victory shout
We know without a doubt
Our God is able

A song like "You Are Holy" is worship. It is vertical; it speaks directly to God from the basis of a one–to–one relationship with Him.

You Are Holy

Lord of the heavens
The earth is in Your hands
You created all completely
With only Your command
Mighty rushing waters
Can never compare to Your voice

I will never know
Why You choose to dwell
In this earthen vessel
Tongue can never tell
Just how great
And awesome that You are

You are holy, holy
Worthy of all glory
There is only one God

19

Praise and worship begin with the words we speak. The Psalmist David said, **"I will bless the Lord at all times: his praise shall continually be in my mouth"** (Ps. 34:1). David said, "Every time I open my mouth, I have two options. I can complain about my situations and my problems or I can praise my way out of my situations and my problems."

Praise and worship are vitally connected to our daily walk. Just because we enter into praise and worship through our music services at church does not mean that is the only time we should praise Him. Praise is a lifestyle of communion with God, based on the words we speak.

We Need To Know Him

Praise is acknowledging what God has done, what He is doing, and what He will do. Praise will tell of God's works and deeds. Often, what others know about Jesus comes straight from our mouths. Our praise, the words we speak, will describe to them a Jesus they can really know.

Worship is acknowledging God for who He is. Worship is all that we are, rightly responding to all that He is. To worship Him, you must know Him.

Jesus, in talking to the Samaritan woman at the well, said that she did not know the God she worshiped, but the Jews did, for salvation was of the Jews. He told her, **"The hour cometh, and now is, when true worshippers shall worship the Father in spirit and in truth . . ."** (John 4:23).

To worship Him **"in spirit and in truth,"** we must know — be intimately acquainted with — the truth.

Jesus said, **"I am the way, the truth, and the life: no man cometh unto the Father, but by me"** (John 14:6). The doorway into the presence of God is a relationship with Jesus Christ.

Suppose a stranger walks up to you and hands you $100. As he walks away, he says, "Meet me here again tomorrow, and I will give you another $100."

You are so excited that you just have to tell somebody. You grab your friend by the shoulders and exclaim, "A man gave me $100 today; he's going to give me $100 again tomorrow!" You are describing the man's actions to your friend; you are praising.

If your friend asks you who the man is, you can't tell him. You don't know. You can praise the man all day long. "He gave me $100. I needed $100. He's going to give me $100 tomorrow." But you can't tell anyone who he is. You don't know him.

This is where many in the church fall short. It's very easy to come into church and praise God while we are all together. It's easy to thank God for something He has done for us, or something we want Him to do. When it comes to worship, though, we must know Him personally.

I truly believe that we are the generation destined for the experiential manifestation of the glory of God — we are going to see God's glory, not just talk about it. That will happen when the church begins to know God, and to worship Him for who He is.

Praise and Worship Are Different

Praise and worship are separate, going two different directions and accomplishing two different things. It's like the difference between authority and power. Consider the old farmer who owned land the state wanted to use for a new road. The surveyors from the highway department came out said, "We're going to put a road through here. We have a petition signed by the governor of this state that gives us the authority to come over here and do this. We don't even have to ask you about it." The old farmer, chewing on a piece of straw, just scratched his head, looked at them and said, "Well, go ahead. Stake it out. No problem."

While the survey crew took out their measuring equipment, the old farmer slipped over to one of his gates and lifted the latch. The old bull that he kept in that pasture came charging out. As the crewmen went running in fear from the fields, the old farmer shouted after them, "Show him your papers! Show the bull your papers!" There is a difference between having the authority to do something and having the power to carry it out.

If we don't know the difference, we can't get the job done. The same is true for praise and worship. If we don't know the difference between praise and worship, we are not going to be able to accomplish what we need to accomplish. We won't really know what we are doing, or what should be happening when we do it.

Magnify the Lord

David said, "O magnify the Lord with me . . ." (Ps. 34:3). When an object is magnified, it appears bigger. With a magnifying glass, we can begin to see all the minute details of what we are studying.

We are not changing what we are looking at. We are just able to see parts that we didn't even know existed before. When we magnify God, we are not changing God — we are changing our perception of Him.

What David meant when he said, "**Magnify the Lord with me,**" was that as we focused our attention on God, we would begin to see more of Him. We would begin to see more of the intricate details and the intimate characteristics of God. We would begin to see more of who God is and what He wants to be in our lives.

What if we could create a food that would cause us to lose weight every time we ate it? Imagine eating something all day and all night and waking up ten pounds lighter the next day — especially if it tasted like pizza or chocolate! Wouldn't that be great?

Of course, there is no natural food that will do that, but there is something we can digest in the spirit that will create and guarantee victory in our lives every day. Praising and magnifying God every day will always bring victory.

Two people can be in the same adversity of life, yet one will receive victory and one will not. The one who does not choose to magnify God will stay right where he is, in the midst of all his problems and trials. The one who magnifies God will see God becoming bigger and bigger in his life.

Magnifying God on a daily basis allows God to become so big in our lives that when troubles come they cannot stay. The more we allow God to fill our lives, the less room there is for trouble.

There is a couple in our church — Tom and Linda Eekfeld — who has adopted a number of severely handicapped children. Most of these children would not have lived without the loving, committed care of these precious people.

We used to live in the same neighborhood. I saw Linda out walking one day, with one baby in a front carrier and two babies in a stroller. I heard my voice coming from the stroller — she had a service tape from church playing!

When I asked her about it, she said that they always have either preaching or praise tapes playing. One of these babies, Bethany, was born without any optic nerves. After daily exposure to this kind of atmosphere, she can see . . . *even though she still doesn't have any optic nerves!*

Another one of their babies, Benjamin, was born with only a brain stem. Babies born with his condition do not have much of a chance for life. But Ben's brain is beginning to grow. *It is not supposed to happen — but it is happening!* This couple — Tom and Linda — has been careful to maintain an atmosphere of praise in their home, with wonderful results.

There are many babies born with these and similar conditions who do not have any hope. Without the intervention of God in their young lives, they will probably die. What makes the difference?

Tom and Linda have chosen to look beyond their babies' many problems toward the answers they know God has for them. They are looking toward a God they have magnified in their own lives, a God who is bigger than all their problems. Praise has made the difference.

We've Come To Magnify

We've come to magnify
We've come to glorify
We've come to lift Him high
The King of kings
We've come to praise His name

No other name ever given to us
Is greater on earth or above
At the sound of that name
Walls of darkness must crumble
Our enemy's defeated as we lift Him up

Daily Victory

David was a perpetual man of war. He said, **"I will bless the Lord at all times: his praise shall continually be in my mouth"** (Ps. 34:1). David realized that the battle he faced yesterday was not the battle he was going to face tomorrow. I have victory now, but I don't know what I will face tomorrow. I will encourage myself in the Lord today and praise Him in preparation for tomorrow. (1 Sam. 30:6.)

Many times, we are walking along in life and all is well, until sudden tragedy strikes. And what is our response?

"Please God, take care of this. Oh God, I thank You for taking care of this. I praise You, Lord. I magnify You, Lord. Come on kids, we are all going to church tonight. I need some results from God."

We have neglected to lay a foundation of praise in the good times, but we want God to respond right now anyway. But God wants to take up residence in a house that is constantly flowing in worship and praise. We won't have to call for Him, He will already be there!

Many times Christians wake up cursing the problems of today, not realizing that they grew from seeds planted yesterday. They do not magnify God on a daily basis; therefore, they don't have daily victories. But God wants us to live in absolute total victory, every day.

But do you know what really excites God? It's when we say, "I believe God is going to do this tomorrow." Then we are saying, "God, we can't see it yet, but we believe that You are able to take us through tomorrow." That is faith.

God responds to faith. We can take the direction of our conversation one of two ways: "My glass is half empty" or "My glass is half full." When we focus our attention on the victory, our praise becomes faith, and God always responds. It's all in the way we look at it.

We're Going Through

We're going through
We will prevail
We're going through
To storm the gates of hell
So when the spirits of darkness
Try to come against you
Remember you're a child of the King
And we're going through

Check Up on Yourself

God will be as great in our lives as our praise allows. Our praise will describe and honor His awesome works in our lives. We can determine our destiny through our praise.

The devil gets a lot of credit for what we produce with our words. He can only respond to what we say — he can't respond to what we think. That's why **"death and life are in the power of the tongue . . ."** (Prov. 18:21). That's why we need to check up on what we are saying.

A young boy walked into a grocery store to use the telephone. He picked up the phone and called his family doctor.

"Doctor, do you need anybody to cut your grass?"

"Well, son," the doctor answered, "no, I don't."

"Are you sure?"

"Yes, I'm sure," the doctor replied. "I already have a young man cutting my grass."

"Is he doing a good job?"

"Well, yes, son," the doctor answered, "he's doing a good job."

"Okay, thank you," the boy said as he hung up the phone.

The clerk who was working at the store looked at the little boy and felt sorry for him.

"Son, if you need a job," the clerk said, "I can let you sweep here at the store. You can come in and help me any time you want, and I'll pay you for it."

The little boy just grinned at him and said, "Oh, I don't need a job."

The clerk was confused. "Didn't I just hear you ask the doctor for a job?"

"No, sir," replied the boy.

"Didn't you just ask him if anybody was cutting his grass?"

"Yes," the boy answered with a nod.

"Didn't you just ask him if the boy that was cutting his grass was doing a good job?"

Again the boy said, "Yes."

"Well, what did you mean?"

The little boy answered, "I'm the boy who cuts his grass. I'm just checking up on myself!"

It's good to check up on ourselves from time to time. It's good to sit down and ask ourselves, "Is there any area in which I'm not experiencing victory? What have I been saying? What have I been talking about? What kind of words have been coming out of my mouth? Have I been offering praise to God?"

We must purpose in our hearts that every time we open our mouths, praise will come out. We can make the decision to let praise flow continually from our mouths . . . and watch the power of God come alive in our lives.

2

Presents. . .or. . .Presence?

Praise always makes a difference.

It is impossible to praise God daily in every situation and be depressed. *Impossible.*

But do you know what the problem with some Christians is? They want to be depressed!

Now why would someone want to be depressed?

There is an old saying that *"misery loves company."* A depressed person will draw a crowd. Have you ever noticed that? "What's wrong, brother? What's wrong? Is everything okay?" they ask. Well–wishers attract onlookers, and it creates a crowd.

People will be attracted to one of two things: they will either be attracted to depression, or they will be attracted to victory. If depression will attract a crowd, how much more will praise and victory attract a crowd?

If someone walks around depressed, they will find a certain crowd of people who will constantly cater to their depression. That person will begin to feed on the attention factor. They will begin to act each day in the way that draws that attention. If it's depression, they will tend to be depressed every day of their life.

The opposite is also true. A person full of the energy and life of God will also draw a crowd. How do they get that way? *Praise!*

The body of Christ is learning. Instead of saying, "Oh, you poor thing," we are saying, "Hey, it's going to be all right. God did this for me. He can do it for you. Let's praise Him together."

Praise Is Contagious

In Exodus, we read about a woman named Miriam, a prophetess, the sister of Moses and Aaron. The Bible says,

> "[She] **took a timbrel in her hand; and all the women went out after her with timbrels and with dances. And Miriam answered them, Sing ye to the Lord, for he hath triumphed gloriously; the horse and his rider hath he thrown into the sea.**"

Exodus 15:20–21

In this passage, we find Miriam praising God for the deliverance of the children of Israel from the hands of the Egyptians. The Bible says they came through on dry ground, and the pursuing Egyptians were all drowned.

Moses began to recount the glorious victory they had experienced. Miriam didn't wait for someone else to lead the way in praise. She took up a tambourine and began to sing and dance and praise God.

Everyone who was there that day enjoyed the same victory that Miriam enjoyed. Everyone who was there had the same opportunity to praise God that Miriam had. Everyone had the same sigh of relief when they began to see God's awesome works.

But this is typical of what happens in the body of Christ. We can be in the middle of a dynamic praise service, experiencing a dynamic move of God, with the same opportunity for victory. Why is it then that so few really seem to have victory? It is because so few choose to really praise.

When we glorify the problems and the trials in our lives, we are inviting those around us to share in those problems. When we glorify the solution, we not only allow God to bring about victory in our lives, but we are providing an answer for the problems of those around us as well.

So many times, people have problems that seem to have no solutions. But there is a solution to every problem — through praise. When we begin to operate in a spirit of praise, things will change. It doesn't make any difference what we are going through, or what we are experiencing. If we will praise God, solutions will come forth, and things will change.

When Miriam began to praise the Lord for the victory that they experienced, **"all the women went out after her with timbrels and with dances"** (Ex. 15:20).

Praise is contagious. If someone would begin to play the piano, the drums, or another instrument, and someone would begin to sing a song of praise, something would begin to happen. Praise is contagious. If someone leads in praise, people will follow in praise.

In Everything Give Thanks

Many times we categorize praise as singing — "When we go to church, we praise Him." Praise can be expressed by singing. But we can praise Him when we wake up in the morning. We can praise Him when we are on the job. We can praise Him wherever we are, or whatever we are doing. We have countless opportunities to give a testimony of what God is doing in our lives.

Clint Brown relates this incident . . .

"About two years ago, my little five–year–old nephew died. It was my brother's little boy. When I arrived at the funeral home, my brother was standing beside the casket.

"I walked up to him and put my arm around him. I thought I was feeling some of the same things he was feeling, and I just didn't know what to say.

"With tears in my eyes, I looked at him and said, 'You know, Greg, I understand what you're going through. We've been praying for you. God's going to take care of this situation and it will be all right.'

"He looked at me so funny as if to say, 'Why are you saying this?' But he just smiled and said, 'I know everything's all right.'

"It really aggravated me, because I wanted him to be down. I wanted him to be depressed. That's what I expected. I wanted him to feel like I was feeling.

"I'm in the ministry, and he's not — and I felt ashamed of myself.

"He said, 'Clint, I don't walk with God or serve God because of how my family is today or how they will be tomorrow. I serve God because He's always going to be God. I serve God because He's never going to change.'

"The experience of hearing him praise God under these circumstances will be in my life forever. But I don't feel the emotion today that I felt that day.

"'Clint, you're hard. Aren't you sorry that your little nephew's not here?' Yes, I am sorry that he's not here. But what I am saying is that I don't feel the depressing, weeping loss now. My brother's words showed me that praise will make a difference."

The things that we face each day are going to change. Emotions can change as circumstances change.

Praise based on emotion is not really praise. It's time for us to grow up and be strong in praise — to resist the devil and to trust God.

The Battle Is the Lord's

It's time to rise up
And then we'll stand up
We're going to put our finger
In the devil's face and say "Shut up"

So keep your head up
Don't think of giving up
Just keep on going strong
For when the war is raging on
You'll never stand alone

The battle is the Lord's

Praise Is More Than Presents

Have you ever watched a young child at Christmas?

As each present is opened, you hear squeals of laughter and excitement. "Oh, thank you! Thank you! It's just what I wanted!"

Then the package is laid aside with the question, "What's next?" And they go on to the next present.

That's the way we act toward God. So often, we come to church with one thing on our minds — our own need.

This is what I'm going to praise God for. I'm going to offer up my sacrifice of praise so God will do this for me."

The next time we come to church, we are praising God for something else. We think God is a big Santa Claus with lots of presents for us. We thank Him, and go on to the next present.

But God wants us to have a relationship with Him. God doesn't want us to walk in emotion. He wants us to walk in experience, living in His presence. He wants us to develop a lifestyle of praise.

Praise is not an emotional high when we are overwhelmed by the blessings we receive. That is not praise; it is emotion.

Praise is not emotion. Praise is experience. Emotions can change from day to day, but an experience lasts forever.

If our praise is based on emotion, we will quickly become bored when the praise service ends and it is time for teaching. We want the emotional high. We will become bored and will not make the sacrifice to learn anything.

The Sacrifice of Praise

We don't know about sacrifice in this country. The ungodly affluence of the world has crept into the church. We don't want to put forth the sacrifice of praise because we live so much in the realm of emotion. If it feels good, do it. If it doesn't, don't.

We only want to praise when we feel like it. But the Bible tells us in Hebrews 13:15, **"By him therefore let us offer the sacrifice of praise to God continually, that is, the fruit of our lips giving thanks to his name."**

Praise is audible. Praise is expression. Praise is action. Praise is acknowledging and accepting someone's performance in your life, or action in your life, and being grateful for it. When we accept God's works, and are thankful for them, we can begin to praise Him.

People are moved by statistics, not sacrifice. When we go somewhere, we send our "bio" ahead of us. "I pastor 8,000 people. I have ministered in 50 countries. I have preached to 750 million people. I have seen 500 million saved."

We are interested in statistics. We think that if we don't have these statistics, our lives have no value.

Moses stood on the mountain and asked, "God, who shall I say sent me?"

God answered, "I AM." (Ex. 3:13–14.)

He could have said, "Moses, tell them I AM the One who carved the earth into being. Moses, tell them I AM the One who threw the sunshine into the air. Moses, tell them I AM the One who hung the stars. Moses, tell them I AM the One who created them. Moses, tell them I AM the One who put the breath in their bodies."

But He didn't say that. He simply said, "I AM."

What does "I AM" mean? It means "You're not." God, through Moses, declared to Pharaoh, "I AM God. You are not God. You are not going to hold these people, because I AM going to set them free. You are not more powerful than I AM."

And He proved it, didn't He?

People are moved by statistics; God is moved by sacrifice. God is not impressed with the statistics of someone who has pastored so many thousands, or preached in so many countries, or has seen so many saved. But He is interested in the sacrifice it takes to do all of these things.

We are interested in the statistics, but God is pleased by the sacrifice. David said, **"Let them sacrifice the sacrifices of thanksgiving, and declare his works with rejoicing"** (Ps. 107:22).

Sacrifice isn't sacrifice until you feel the loss. Sacrifice doesn't take place until you feel something leave.

We think praise is telling God what we've done for Him that day. How many times have you heard a statement like this: "When I was growing up, I walked barefoot eight miles in the snow just to get to church"? We thought it was what we accomplished that praised God.

Praise is not what *we* have done; it is what *God* has done. Praise is not acknowledging *our* works; praise is acknowledging *His* works. It is not for what we accomplish that we praise Him; it is for what He has accomplished through us that we praise Him.

And For His Pleasure

There are many Christians who know little about their purpose on earth. They know only that they need to be saved so they can go to heaven. Every song they sing is about heaven. All their preaching is about going to hell or going to heaven.

It is true we need to come back to some strong preaching about a heaven to gain and a hell to shun. But if God's only purpose for us was to take us to heaven after we are saved, wouldn't He have done it already? Wouldn't His purpose be complete when we were saved?

God created us to praise Him. **"Thou art worthy, O Lord, to receive glory and honour and power: for thou hast created all things, and for thy pleasure they are and were created"** (Rev. 4:11). God created man as the apex of His creation, and man's purpose was to give God pleasure.

First Peter 2:9 says,

> **"Ye are a chosen generation, a royal priesthood, an holy nation, a peculiar people; that ye should shew forth the praises of him who hath called you out of darkness into his marvellous light."**

God called us out of darkness into light to praise Him. God took us from where we were and put us into the light for a purpose — to glorify Him, to magnify Him, to lift Him up, to be an example for Him. We are walking testimonies of what God can do. God wants us to show forth His marvelous works through our praise, through what we say, and through what we do.

Judah Shall Plow

Brother Clint once asked his uncle, a farmer, about plowing.

"How important is the depth of the plow?" he asked.

"It makes all the difference," his uncle replied. "If the seed is planted too deep, it won't get enough water. If it's not deep enough, the roots won't be able to grow. The right depth is everything."

An understanding of the role of praise and worship is essential. Praise is more than a superficial singing of songs; it is an instrument in the hands of a believer. Praise is a plow; it prepares the soil — the hearts of the people — to receive the Word of God.

The tribe of Judah — which means praise — was given the responsibility to go before the Israelites to secure victory in the Promised Land. (Judg. 1.)

Hosea the prophet said,

"... **Judah shall plow, and Jacob shall break his clods. Sow to yourselves in righteousness, reap in mercy; break up your fallow ground: for it is time to seek the Lord, till he come and rain righteousness upon you.**"

Hosea 10:11–12

Praise builds an altar. We offer ourselves to God on that altar — the **"sacrifice of praise . . . the fruit of our lips giving thanks to his name"** (Heb. 13:15). We till up the ground of our hearts so God can plant seeds into our lives today — for tomorrow's victory.

Zion Keeps Calling Me

Zion keeps calling me
To a higher place of praise
To stand upon the mountain
And magnify His Name
To tell all the people
And every nation that He reigns
Zion keeps calling me
To a higher place of praise

A Throne of Dominion

"**I will praise thee, O Lord, among the people: I will sing unto thee among the nations. For thy mercy is great unto the heavens, and thy truth unto the clouds. Be thou exalted, O God, above the heavens: let thy glory be above all the earth.**"

Psalm 57:9–11

Praise releases the authority of God into our lives as we exalt Him. Praise says to God, "Sit down upon the throne that I build You. Take the weapon of my praise in Your hands and destroy my enemies, and break the awful power of the devil in my life. I give You that seat of authority. Take the reins of my life, Lord."

God inhabits — comes to dwell in — the praises of His people: **"But thou art holy, O thou that inhabitest the praises of Israel"** (Ps. 22:3).

God said He would be with us in times of trouble, sitting on the throne of our praise.

> **"He shall call upon me, and I will answer him: I will be with him in trouble; I will deliver him, and honour him. With long life will I satisfy him, and shew him my salvation."**

> **Psalm 91:15–16**

Learn to worship God in the midnight hour. Paul and Silas did.

> **"And at midnight Paul and Silas prayed, and sang praises unto God: and the prisoners heard them.**

> **"And suddenly there was a great earthquake, so that the foundations of the prison were shaken: and immediately all the doors were opened, and every one's bands were loosed."**

> **Acts 16:25–26**

When the demonic forces of the adversary rise up against us, we build God's throne a little higher. We exalt Him, building His throne higher and higher.

No situation in our lives is bigger than the throne of God. A lack of praise, adoration, and worship gives the opposing forces of the enemy a higher place of dominion in our lives than the level to which we have exalted Jesus. That is how the devil is able to exert dominion in our lives.

"Pastor, it's too late. The devil is already breathing down my neck!" The Bible tells us to redeem the time, for the days are evil. (Eph. 5:16.) We can take back what the devil has stolen. That's the reason David tells us to bless the Lord at all times — in order to have a continuous flow of praise to God, creating a hedge of protection around us.

"I thought God was already exalted." God has already exalted the Lord Jesus Christ and given Him a name which is above every name. (Phil. 2:9.) **"Unto the Son he saith, Thy throne, O God, is for ever and ever: a sceptre of righteousness is the sceptre of thy kingdom"** (Heb. 1:8).

It remains for us to exalt Him in our lives. There is a difference between Jesus being Savior and Jesus being Lord. God has already exalted Jesus and given Him dominion. When we build Him a throne of praise, we are giving Him lordship — a place of dominion.

Every day of our lives we can find new areas over which to give Him dominion. We must build a throne of praise in that area so He can rule and reign from the place of authority we give Him. We must release that dominion to Him.

God sits on the throne of praise we build. He looks at the devil and all of his striving against us, and He begins to laugh. **"He that sitteth in the heavens shall laugh: the Lord shall have them in derision"** (Ps. 2:4). He knows the devil is powerless in the face of the praises of God's people.

What does the Bible say?

"If the goodman of the house had known in what watch the thief would come, he would have watched, and would not have suffered his house to be broken up."

Matthew 24:43

The adversary is coming. We must set guards on the wall of our houses. He has his arsenal of disease, defeat, discouragement, dismay, and dissatisfaction. He will try to cause us to question the Word of God, the love of God, and the power of God in our lives. He is coming . . . are we ready?

The way to be ready is to praise and exalt God, building Him a throne of authority before the devil comes in sight. Exalt God, magnify Him, and find that high place.

We can dwell continually in that high place, the secret place of habitation in God. **"He that dwelleth in the secret place of the most High shall abide under the shadow of the Almighty"** (Ps. 91:1).

It is God's desire that we live in the place of constant, continual communion with Him. That place of communion becomes our ark of safety against all the wiles of our enemy.

It Feels So Good When I Praise Him

It feels so good when I praise Him
It feels so good lifting Him up
Strongholds must go
When we praise in one accord
It feels so good just praising the Lord

We're going to lift Him higher
Higher, higher, higher
It feels so good just praising the Lord

3

Bible Ways To Praise the Lord

We are a people determined to praise God today. We are striving to walk in maturity in our praise. We are coming to the house of God to worship Him. If the President were sitting on the front row or if the Pope came in the side door, it wouldn't change our focus. God will withhold nothing from a people who will praise Him with their whole heart.

Athletes run up and down a field kicking a dead pigskin, while thousands of fans leap up, cheer, and throw their cola or beer all over each other because their team made a touchdown. *No one thinks that is excessive!*

Crowds shout and yell at a boxing match, as they watch one man beat another man almost to death. *No one thinks that is excessive!*

Teenagers scream and nearly faint when their rock star idols begin to sing and gyrate to the beat of their top–of–the–chart songs. *No one thinks that is excessive!*

Yet the church is looked down upon for glorifying the God of their salvation with their whole heart, mind, soul, and strength and for glorifying the God who turned them from a life spent going toward hell and placed them on the road to a place called heaven.

The criticisms ring out: "I just don't know what would cause someone to act like that. We don't do it that way in our denomination. I just don't believe that's proper."

But their denomination didn't save them, and their denomination didn't heal them. Their denomination didn't give them joy when they didn't have any.

"**For these are not drunken, as ye suppose, seeing it is but the third hour of the day**" (Acts 2:15). They have found something stronger than anything they could shoot in their arms or find in a bottle. "**But this is that which was spoken by the prophet Joel**" (Acts 2:16).

What would make someone want to dance across the front of a sanctuary? What would make someone want to lift their hands and shout praises to God, with tears streaming down their face?

Who would act that way?

I can tell you who. It's the hopeless alcoholic who was on his way to hell before God delivered him. It's the helpless drug addict with nothing to live for until God gave her new life and new hope. It's any man or woman who has known the saving, healing, delivering touch of a God who is bigger than they are. They want to express their joy and thankfulness to the God who set them free!

What makes them act like that? They believe in the supernatural. What makes them act like that? They believe in miracles. What makes them act like that? They believe in healing. What makes them act like that? They believe Jesus is coming again!

There was a young teenage boy dancing before the Lord at the altar during one of our Sunday services. He was totally consumed with expressing himself to the Lord, and it was beautiful to behold.

Wouldn't you rather see a young man acting like that in church than to see him out on the streets dancing to the beat of the world? Wouldn't you rather see him have a preacher for a hero than some drug dealer? Wouldn't you rather see him turned on by God than by crack cocaine?

This is what the world needs to see. God said,

"**And it shall come to pass in the last days, saith God, I will pour out of my Spirit upon all flesh: and your** sons and your daughters shall prophesy, and your young men shall see visions, and your old men shall dream dreams."

Acts 2:17

There is enough for everyone.

It has nothing to do with economic status. It has nothing to do with social status. It has to do with only one thing: they have been to the spout where the glory comes out! They have been touched by God.

God will anoint us to praise Him. Praise is a commandment: **"Let every thing that hath breath praise the Lord. Praise ye the Lord"** (Ps. 150:6).

The commandments of God are not optional, and they are not flexible. It's time to get radically fanatical about the God we say we serve.

Our praise and worship are not to please us, neither are they to please those around us. They are for God. They are to please Him. It pleases God when we act in faith and act on His Word. (Heb. 11:6.)

Our praise and worship are not to try to "get something." They are because we already have something! They come from a heart of love overflowing with thanksgiving for all that God is and for all that He has done.

How much has God done for us? Enough that we want to praise Him for it? Enough to lay aside our own preconceived ideas and worship God the way the Bible instructs?

The Scriptures overflow with instructions on how to praise God. There are many examples of what happened when God's people praised Him. We must make the decision. We must decide within ourselves if God is worthy of our praise.

43

Clap Your Hands

"O clap your hands, all ye people . . ." (Ps. 47:1).

Religion wants us to be quiet.

Religious tradition seeks to make us ignorant of our authority — and the source of that authority. Jesus had a right to authority here because He came in through the door of the flesh. Jesus was born of a woman into this earth realm; Satan was not. Therefore, Satan has no legitimate authority in this earth.

John 10:1–2 says,

"Verily, verily, I say unto you, He that entereth not by the door into the sheepfold, but climbeth up some other way, the same is a thief and a robber. But he that entereth in by the door is the shepherd of the sheep."

Jesus said, **"All power is given unto me in heaven and in earth. Go ye therefore . . ."** (Matt. 28:18–19).

Jesus transferred His authority to us.

This is why we clap our hands — it is the sound of flesh on flesh, demonstrating our authority in the earth.

Clap your hands!

Arise

Arise, He's already won the war
Arise, there's nothing to go back for
Don't back up, don't hesitate
The time is now to demonstrate
The victory of Our Lord
So church, arise

We are just a mirror reflection
Of a mighty God that's resurrected
He's placed His awesome power in our hands
We are living in the dispensation
The time is now for demonstration
The fallen angel must obey our command

Shout His Praise!

"...shout unto God with the voice of triumph" (Ps. 47:1).

What does shouting have to do with praise?

The book of Ezra records the restoration of worship when the Israelites returned from exile. Through a proclamation by Cyrus, king of Persia, authorization was given to rebuild the temple which had been destroyed.

"And when the builders laid the foundation of the temple of the Lord, they set the priests in their apparel with trumpets, and the Levites the sons of Asaph with cymbals, to praise the Lord, after the ordinance of David king of Israel.

"And they sang together by course in praising and giving thanks unto the Lord; because he is good, for his mercy endureth for ever toward Israel. And all the people shouted with a great shout, when they praised the Lord, because the foundation of the house of the Lord was laid."

Ezra 3:10–11

They knew that when the temple was rebuilt and worship was restored God would again dwell among them. They looked forward to the time when God's glory would once more be manifested in their midst.

These are the days of the restoration of scriptural praise and worship to the body of Christ.

After 400 years of silence, the voice of John the Baptist came as one crying in the wilderness, "Prepare ye the way of the Lord" (Matt. 3:3). John had a message from God. He proclaimed it boldly and unashamedly.

We, too, have a message from God. As John the Baptist was commissioned to herald the first coming of Jesus Christ to the earth, so are we commissioned to herald His second coming.

When Jesus made His triumphal entry into Jerusalem, the Bible says "a very great multitude" came out to meet Him. They spread their cloaks before Him and waved palm branches, crying **"Hosanna to the son of David"** (Matt. 21:9). They were shouting because they thought He was coming to set up His earthly kingdom.

Every day, we are drawing closer to His return.

If the Israelites shouted about the rebuilding of the temple, how much more should we be shouting now? God is rebuilding His temple in us! Not only has Jesus made an entrance into our lives, but He will soon make an entrance into this world.

If the multitudes welcomed Jesus' coming into Jerusalem with a shout, how much more should we lift our voices as we see the day of His return approaching?

Shout His praise!

I've Got a Reason to Shout

I've got a reason to shout
I was in darkness, but God brought me out
I'm here to testify and tell you about
My wonderful reason to shout
We've been through the fire
We've been through the flood
He's been by my side
When you've got God
You've got enough

Praise Him With Instruments

"It came even to pass, as the trumpeters and singers were as one, to make one sound to be heard in praising and thanking the Lord; and when they lifted up their voice with the trumpets and cymbals and instruments of musick, and praised the Lord, saying, For he is good; for his mercy endureth for ever: that then the house was

filled with a cloud, even the house of the Lord; So that the priests could not stand to minister by reason of the cloud: for the glory of the Lord had filled the house of God."

2 Chronicles 5:13–14

As early as the seventh generation from Adam, the Bible records the use of instruments among men. There was a man whose name was Jubal, who was **"the father of all such as handle the harp and organ"** (Gen. 4:21).

The use of instruments reflects the creation of Lucifer in the prehistory of the world. His entire being was an instrument of praise to God — **". . . the workmanship of thy tabrets and of thy pipes was prepared in thee in the day that thou wast created"** (Ezek. 28:13) — before he was consumed with pride and cast from the presence of God.

King Saul, when he was troubled by an evil spirit, was advised by his counselors to **"seek out a man, who is a cunning player on an harp . . . that he shall play with his hand, and thou shalt be well"** (1 Sam. 16:16).

David was the man they chose. He played and Saul **"was refreshed, and was well, and the evil spirit departed from him"** (v. 23).

David's psalms were written to be set to music. Many even specify what type of instrument was to be used.

Prophets used instruments of music to receive the word of the Lord. Jehoshaphat, king of Judah, needed some battle strategy information. He sent for Elisha the prophet, who called for a minstrel. **"And it came to pass, when the minstrel played, that the hand of the Lord came upon him. And he said, Thus saith the Lord . . ."** (2 Kings 3:15–16).

John heard instruments of music around the throne of God. **"And I heard a voice from heaven, as the voice of many waters, and as the voice of a great thunder: and I heard the voice of harpers harping with their harps"** (Rev. 14:2).

Instruments are often used to accompany singing. **"Praise the Lord with harp: sing unto him with the psaltery and an instrument of ten strings. Sing unto him a new song; play skillfully with a loud noise"** (Ps. 33:2–3).

From time to time in our services, Brother Clint will direct that certain instruments be played. There is a special anointing that accompanies instruments, often bringing in a tangible anointing of the presence of God and allowing me to hear the direction of God for the service.

God's plan is for everything that has breath to praise Him — we were designed to be instruments of His praise in the earth.

God's purpose is always redemptive. Jesus said, **"And I, if I be lifted up from the earth, will draw all men unto me"** (John 12:32). Our praise dispels the work of our enemy and allows God's presence to be displayed in our midst, drawing our friends and family to Jesus Christ.

Praise Him with instruments!

Cry Aloud

Cry aloud and spare not
Lift up your voice just like a trumpet
Show forth the works of the enemy

Stand up for righteousness
Proclaim that God alone is worthy
Raise high the banner of Our King

He sits high upon His throne
And He's holy alone
There is no God
As big as mine

Sing His Praises

"Sing praises to God, sing praises: sing praises unto our King, sing praises" (Ps. 47:6).

The greatest of all instruments is the human voice. With the voice, the Gospel can be preached; and men and women, boys and girls, can be led to the Lord.

We do not sing songs just to take up time. Singing songs of praise and worship brings us into the presence of God. David said, **"Enter into his gates with thanksgiving, and into his courts with praise . . ."** (Ps. 100:4).

Singing as a form of praise is evident throughout the Bible. From the time of the children of Israel's release from captivity until the saints are gathered around the throne in glory, singing can be seen as a vehicle of praise.

We have already looked at Miriam's song of praise and deliverance. Remember how she began to sing and dance and all the ladies followed her example?

Singing was such an important part of worship in New Testament times that Paul even gave instructions for its use. **"I will sing with the spirit,"** he said, **"and I will sing with the understanding also"** (1 Cor. 14:15).

He also told them to keep themselves full of the Spirit, speaking to themselves in **"psalms and hymns and spiritual songs, singing and making melody in your heart to the Lord"** (Eph. 5:19).

In the book of Revelation, John sees a preview of the redeemed saints praising around the throne of God:

> **"And they sung a new song, saying, Thou art worthy to take the book, and to open the seals thereof: for thou wast slain, and hast redeemed us to God by thy blood out of every kindred, and tongue, and people, and nation."**

> **Revelation 5:9**

When Jesus made His entry back into Jerusalem, the crowds were vocal in their praise, crying, **"Blessed be the King that cometh in the name of the Lord"** (Luke 19:38). The Pharisees came to Jesus and told Him to rebuke them. Jesus said, **"If these should hold their peace, the stones would immediately cry out"** (v. 40).

I don't know about you, but I don't want a rock to take my place in praising and worshiping my King!

Sing His praises!

Lift Up Your Praise

Lift up your praise
For your song belongs to Him
Let the earth come before Him and rejoice
There is no strength that is greater than His joy
Lift up your praise unto the Lord

Alleluia, Thine the glory
Alleluia, Amen
Alleluia, Thine the glory
Lift up your praise unto Him

Lift Up Your Hands

"Lift up your hands in the sanctuary, and bless the Lord" (Ps. 134:2).

Lifting up our hands is a universal sign of surrender. We are letting go of ourselves — reaching for something outside of us that is bigger than we are.

After their deliverance from Egyptian bondage, the children of Israel came to battle with the Amalekites at Rephidim. (Ex. 17.)

Moses gave battle instructions to Joshua. Joshua was to fight with the Amalekites while Moses stood on the top of the hill and lifted up his hands.

While Moses' hands were lifted up, Israel prevailed; when he let down his hands, Amalek prevailed. Aaron and Hur stood on either side of Moses and held his hands up when he grew weary.

Joshua won that battle. Moses built an altar there and called it Jehovah–nissi, which means the Lord, my banner of victory.

"I will therefore that men pray every where, lifting up holy hands, without wrath and doubting" (1 Tim. 2:8).

Holy hands are clean hands. Our hands represent who we are. Clean hands and a pure heart speak of holiness. The blessing that comes with holiness is the manifested presence of God in our lives.

Moses lifted his hands toward God, surrendering control of the battle to Him. God manifested Himself on behalf of Moses and gave him victory over the Amalekites. As we walk in holiness and lift our hands in praise and worship to God, we are demonstrating that we have given control of our lives to Him.

As we walk in holiness, we have no cause for wrath and doubting. We have been saved from wrath, and our faith–filled praise banishes any doubts we may have that God will be able to perform His Word.

Lifting our hands reminds us that God is bigger than we are.

I remember praying for a gentleman several years ago; He came to the altar in tears of agony. When I asked him what was wrong, he said, "I want to be able to lift my hands."

"But you have been in church all your life," I responded.

"Yes," he said, "but where I went, we were never allowed to raise our hands. And if we dared, it was only one hand."

We prayed together, and God set him wonderfully free! I will never forget seeing him thrust his hands up in the air and begin to praise the Lord. I don't know when I have ever seen a man get so blessed!

Don't allow anything to keep you from lifting your hands and worshiping God.

Praise Him!

Lift up your hands!

We've Been Called To Battle

We've been called to battle
We are armed and filled with power
Satan, acknowledge this is your final hour
Our forces know the source
Of the power in their hands
Our ammunition is the Spirit
We'll fire at God's command
The praise upon our lips
Shall deal the deadly blow
As we march on to the fight
and conquer every foe
We won't back down
from the spirits of darkness anymore
We are armed and ready
We're going on with the Lord

We will keep fighting, possessing what is ours
We will go forward, we will never die

Praise Him in the Dance

"The Lord thy God in the midst of thee is mighty; he will save, he will rejoice over thee with joy; he will rest in his love, he will joy [pirouette] over thee with singing."

Zephaniah 3:17

"Let Israel rejoice in him that made him: let the children of Zion be joyful [pirouette] in their King. Let them praise his name in the dance: let them sing praises unto him with the timbrel and harp."

Psalm 149:2–3

The word translated in these two verses as *joy* or *joyful* comes from a Hebrew word which means to spin around or to pirouette under the influence of strong emotion.

God rejoices over us with such overwhelming joy that He is spinning around in circles!

And David admonishes God's people to do the same — **"Let the children of Zion be joyful** [pirouette] **in their King."**

He knew what he was talking about.

The Philistines had taken the Ark of the Lord from the children of Israel. They kept it until it proved to be too much for them — they were overtaken by one plague after another while it was in their possession.

So David took an ox cart and went to retrieve the Ark. (2 Sam. 6.) This was the first mistake. The problem was he did not check on the proper way to transport it.

Uzzah, one of David's priests, saw the Ark begin to shake as the oxen pulled the cart and reached out his hand to steady it. This was the second mistake. The Bible says, **"The anger of the Lord was kindled against Uzzah; and God smote him there for his error; and there he died by the ark of God"** (v. 7).

David was afraid of the Ark then, so he decided to leave it where it was — near the house of Obed–edom. Soon, the house of Obed–edom was blessed so abundantly that David realized the Ark belonged in Jerusalem with him.

David went to get the Ark again, this time without incident. They arrived safely in Jerusalem with the Ark. David was thankful, and stopped when they had gone **"six paces"** (v. 13). Six is the number of man — David had come to the end of himself and was ready to focus on God.

David prepared a sacrifice to worship the Lord and **"danced before the Lord with all his might"** (v. 14). God was pleased with David's sacrifice of praise.

Michal, David's wife, was not. The Bible says Michal **"despised him in her heart"** (v. 16). Her attitude had devastating consequences. She became barren, and **"had no child unto the day of her death"** (v. 23).

To despise the move of God is to invite spiritual barrenness. The religious church world has long cast a scornful look at dancing before the Lord . . . and has despised it. The spiritual barrenness produced as a result is evidenced by a lack of fruit. Where are the souls who have been born again because of the testimony of their worship?

Let our hearts always burn with the holy fire of God. Let us always be free to express our thanksgiving and praise to God, and to dance before Him. To worship this way is redemptive. Dance and leap and twirl and spin!

Praise Him in the dance!

Heart of Fire
Heart of fire
Live in me today
As your flame burns bright
Your light I will display

Let Your Word in me remain
Let Your will be my desire

Burn in me, oh heart of fire
Burn in me, oh heart of fire

Give

"And Aaron lifted up his hand toward the people, and blessed them, and came down from offering of the sin offering, and the burnt offering, and peace offerings.

"And Moses and Aaron went into the tabernacle of the congregation, and came out, and blessed the people: and the glory of the Lord appeared unto all the people.

"And there came a fire out from before the Lord, and consumed upon the altar the burnt offering and the fat: which when all the people saw, they shouted, and fell on their faces."

Leviticus 9:22–24

The glory of God is always manifested around sacrifice. God gave specific instructions to Moses regarding the sacrifices that were to be offered in the Old Testament order of worship.

He promised that when they obeyed Him, His presence would be manifested to accept their sacrifices. **"This is the thing which the Lord commanded that ye should do: and the glory of the Lord shall appear unto you"** (Lev. 9:6).

In the tabernacle there was a very formal order of worship established which progressed from the outer court, to the inner court, and on into the Holy of Holies.

The Holy of Holies was a small area enclosed by curtains through which no light could penetrate: it was completely dark. When the priest entered once a year, he made his way to the Ark of the Covenant in the dark. The Hebrews thought of the Ark of the Covenant as the throne of God. They understood that the Ark was the place where God came down to meet with them.

When the priest sprinkled the blood of sacrifice on the mercy seat, the shekinah glory of God — the light unlighted, the light that had no source of origin except in God — split the blackness and illuminated the mercy seat, receiving the sacrifice.

In New Testament practice, there is a carry–over from the Old Testament patterns of worship. The Apostle Paul said, **"What? know ye not that your body is the temple of the Holy Ghost which is in you, which ye have of God, and ye are not your own?"** (1 Cor. 6:19).

The word translated "temple" from the Greek language is *naos*, which means "the central sanctuary," the Holy of Holies.

Paul was saying, "Your body is the Holy of Holies. The mercy seat of God is now enthroned in you." We have become the ark of the Lord, the place where God comes to meet with men.

The lampstand which gave light to the tabernacle was to be made of pure gold, **"after their pattern, which was shewed thee in the mount"** (Ex. 25:40). The bowls of the lampstand were to be filled with **"pure oil olive beaten for the light, to cause the lamp to burn always"** (Ex. 27:20).

Praise and worship were offered continually at the tabernacle, and the presence of God was manifested in a very real way. God Himself came down to dwell with His people, and to meet all of their needs.

God wants to fashion His people into a golden bowl of praise and worship into which He can pour His life, **"that the residue of men might seek after the Lord . . ."** (Acts 15:17).

Out of this vessel — the body of Christ — needy people can come and drink, and they will be saved, healed, delivered, and set free.

Do you want the glory of God to be revealed in your life?

Do you want revival in your heart? in your family? in your church?

Do you want God to accept the sacrifices you offer Him?

"But isn't our sacrifice now in New Testament times **'the fruit of our lips'**?" (Heb. 13:15). "Isn't it enough of a sacrifice if I praise God when I don't feel like it?"

Let's take a closer look at this passage of Scripture.

> **"By him therefore let us offer the sacrifice of praise to God continually, that is, the fruit of our lips giving thanks to his name. But to do good and to communicate forget not: for with such sacrifices God is well pleased."**
>
> **Hebrews 13:15–16**

Speaking words of praise is important. Words are the vehicle through which the plans and purposes of God come about in the earth. And it certainly is a sacrifice to open our mouths and speak words of praise and thanksgiving when we feel like doing anything but that!

But there is more to it.

"To do good and to communicate forget not." The word communicate refers to alms–giving. The Amplified Bible renders it this way:

> **"Do not forget or neglect to do kindness and good, to be generous and distribute and contribute to the needy [of the church as embodiment and proof of fellowship], for such sacrifices are well pleasing to God."**

Distribute?

Contribute?

Give?

What does giving have to do with worship?

To show God that our heart is really toward Him, we must be givers. Giving seals our worship and tells God that we really believe the words of praise we are speaking!

It tells God where our heart is — **"For where your treasure is, there will your heart be also"** (Matt. 6:21). It takes faith to give, and faith pleases God.

Every year at Easter we take a great Resurrection Seed offering at World Harvest Church. We see more salvations, miracles, and healings during the weeks surrounding this special offering than at any other time during the year.

Coincidence? I don't think so.

Many people give more thought and attention to their giving for this offering than they do ordinarily — so they receive more than they do ordinarily. God said He would show up when we do things His way.

The time is coming when the body of Christ will know how to release themselves in worship to God. His presence will be manifested in such a way that people are going to receive miracles — legs are going to be straightened out, blind eyes are going to be opened, the lame are going to walk — without anybody praying for them or laying hands on them.

Giving is the key!

We can tell the degree of loving by the depth of giving. God reached into the very depths of His being and unbosomed a part of Himself. God so loved the world that He gave . . . the very best He had.

As we give, the Christ of the candlesticks and the Lord of the lampstands will be manifested in our midst. Everyone who comes into the house of God will be blessed as a result.

Give!

One Drop of Blood

One drop of blood that day
Was enough for humanity
On a hill, the victory wrought
The price was paid
With just one drop

His blood
Still healing the hurt and diseased
His blood
Still flows as a cleansing stream
His blood
A rushing river of grace
His blood

4

The Valuable Vessel

"And, behold, a woman in the city, which was a sinner, when she knew that Jesus sat at meat in the Pharisee's house, brought an alabaster box of ointment,

"And stood at his feet behind him weeping, and began to wash his feet with tears, and did wipe them with the hairs of her head, and kissed his feet, and anointed them with ointment."

Luke 7:37–38

This woman, who was known to be a sinner, came to the table where Jesus was eating. She began to weep and wash His feet with her tears, drying them with her hair. She broke open the alabaster box of ointment she had with her and used it to anoint His feet.

The Pharisee began to explain to Jesus how valuable this oil was and who this woman was — he couldn't believe that Jesus would allow a woman with a past like hers to do such a thing.

Jesus said, "I want to tell you about two men. One man had a large debt and the other had a small debt. Neither man had the money to pay his debt, but their creditor forgave them both. Tell me, which man will love him the most?"

He answered, "It must be the man who owed the most."

"You are absolutely right," Jesus said. "The man who has been forgiven the most will love the most. This woman loves me, and sacrificed greatly to show it, but you haven't done anything!"

When the woman came to Jesus, she used the most valuable thing she possessed to worship Him. The ointment represented an investment of a great sum of money, perhaps as much as a year's wages.

The Pharisee recognized the cost of what this woman was doing and saw it as waste. In his day, the feet were the dirtiest part of a person's body.

They didn't wear shoes and walk on sidewalks as you and I do. They walked in sandals through dusty streets that were often scattered with animal droppings.

To wash someone else's feet was a sign of servitude and great humility. Why waste such costly goods for so menial a task?

The night before He was betrayed, Jesus washed His disciples' feet. They objected, knowing that their feet, being always so exposed, were the dirtiest part of their bodies.

But that was the very part Jesus wanted to cleanse — the part that was exposed. Jesus told them, "I want to wash your feet. I want to cleanse you where you need it most."

When we come into the house of God, we lay our worship at Jesus' feet. We expose ourselves to His scrutiny. We begin to anoint His feet with our worship. Through our praise and worship, we begin to declare who Jesus is and what He has done in our lives.

Pouring Out the Oil

Many times when we come to worship, we bring with us the problems that we've gone through during the day — the dirt and the pollution of the world — and a lot of us are still thinking about them.

We must come willing to lay it all down at Jesus' feet. "Lord, we want You to wash us of everything that we've gone through this week and everything we've gone through today; we want it cleansed from us."

Jesus also recognized the cost of what the woman was doing. But He understood that her worship had a value far beyond the price of the ointment. She did not offer that which cost her nothing.

As the woman knew, it was not just the container which was valuable but what was inside it.

We are that vessel which must be broken before worship can be released. We must start looking at what is inside our vessel.

Boxes of ointment such as this woman used were carefully preserved. The containers were frequently checked and their contents evaluated. They knew that there would come a time when they would need to use what was inside.

What are we releasing from the inside of us? Before we minister to others, we have a responsibility to evaluate our vessel. What we are on the inside will be poured out on the people.

Is it holy? Is it valuable? Is it pure?

The Pharisee thought it was a waste for the woman to pour her costly oil on Jesus' dirty feet. If we are not careful, we can have the same attitude. "These people! They are lucky to have me at this church. They are lucky to have my talents and abilities here."

What we are really saying is this: "Jesus, Your feet are too dirty for me to get excited about pouring oil on them. Don't expect me to get too excited about pouring my valuable talent on Your dirty feet."

"But you're talking about ministering to Jesus. I thought we were talking about ministering to others?"

We are!

In every situation there are those who are bound and in prison. There are people who are hungry for something to fill the emptiness in their lives. There are people who are alone and feel like no one cares about them or their needs.

Jesus said,

"For I was an hungred, and ye gave me meat: I was thirsty, and ye gave me drink: I was a stranger, and ye took me in:

"Naked, and ye clothed me: I was sick, and ye visited me: I was in prison, and ye came unto me.

"Then shall the righteous answer him, saying, Lord, when saw we thee an hungred, and fed thee? or thirsty, and gave thee drink?

"When saw we thee a stranger, and took thee in? or naked, and clothed thee? Or when saw we thee sick, or in prison, and came unto thee?"

[Jesus answered them,] "Inasmuch as ye have done it unto one of the least of these my brethren, ye have done it unto me."

Matthew 25:35–40

When we minister to others, we are ministering to Him.

Our worth to God in public depends upon what we are in private. How can we worship God in public if we don't worship Him in private?

Sometimes the Lord wakes me up in the middle of the night and says, "Dance before Me." I don't know about you, but crawling out of bed at 3:30 in the morning isn't easy! No piano, no drums, no trumpets. But it is just as important as our worship in the church.

When we worship God, we are making an investment in our future — we are giving God something to work with. Then, when a time of need arises in our lives, the seeds for victory have already been sown.

Talent and ability are useless to God if He does not have our hearts. If He doesn't have our hearts, He doesn't have any of us. We are as ". . . **sounding brass, or a tinkling cymbal**" (1 Cor. 13:1).

Talent won't take us the distance.

Our relationship with God will take us the distance. It makes all the difference. Worship will flow from our hearts when we know God and have a relationship with Him.

The woman who poured her oil on Jesus' feet knew who she was and who Jesus was. She worshiped Him not out of a sense of duty, but because she knew Him, and who He was to her. And it paved the way for what Jesus said to her — **"Thy sins are forgiven"** — and brought great victory into her life. (Lk. 7:37–50.)

Coming Face to Face

Brother Clint was involved in a serious accident which brought him face to face with the necessity for this kind of relationship with God.

"One Thursday evening I told my wife, Angie, that I was going over to the gym at World Harvest Church to run and to shoot some basketball. It was about 6:00 when I came through the corridor and passed by the sanctuary doors.

"The Holy Ghost began to tug at my heart, so I went in, turned all the power on, and sat down at the keyboard. I began to sing songs of praise and worship to God. As I worshiped Him, I began to weep and pray.

"'God, no matter what it takes, get me to the place where I know that I know You. Get me to the place where I know why I'm here and how to lead this congregation into Your presence. Whatever it takes, God.'

"I thought I was alone, but I was wrong. A dear lady who had been cleaning the sanctuary was sitting nearby. When I turned around and saw her, it startled me. She said to me, 'I've never felt the presence of God in a place like I feel it right now.'

"That was Thursday. The next morning, I got up, put my suit on, and left for the church at about 7:30. It was an icy day, very cold and wet.

"I could count on one hand the times I have ever worn a seat belt . . . but that morning, I put it on.

"A young woman was on her way to World Harvest Bible Institute, which is between my house and the church. As she came up over a small hill about a mile from the school, she skidded on a patch of ice. Her car came left of center and hit my van head–on.

"I was thrown into the windshield and back into my seat. My seat belt held long enough to keep me from going through the windshield and then snapped from the force of the impact.

"I couldn't feel my legs. I was dazed. Blood was running down my face. I was trying to get out of the van and thought maybe my legs were pinned somehow. I looked down, and they weren't — but I couldn't move them.

"I couldn't get my door open, so I pulled myself over and tried the passenger door. The van had come to rest on an embankment, so when I managed to get the door open, I fell out and rolled down into a ditch.

"As I lay there on the ground — soaking wet, with snow falling on my face, unable to move my legs — God began to speak to me. He reminded me of the three hours I had spent praising, worshiping, and communing with Him the night before.

"It made me stop and think. God said, 'What is going to get you through this is not your ability, not your gifting, not your talent — it's your relationship with Me.'

"And I found out on the ground that day that worship goes beyond singing a song. It goes beyond writing a song. I realized that day that neither my ability, my gifting, nor my talent will ever supersede the relationship I have with Him. *Nothing God has given me will ever be more valuable to me than my relationship with Him.*

"I had to come to the point inside that day that I could say, 'God, no matter what happens — if I never walk again, if I never play the piano or sing again, I'm still going to serve You. I'm still going to worship You. I'm still going to do what You have called me to do. I don't worship You for what You've done, or what You're doing, or what You're going to do; I worship You because of Who You are.'

"Worshipping God prepared me for what was ahead; worshipping God took me through it; worshipping God sustains me today."

Standing on the Rock

Standing, standing
Standing on the rock of my salvation
Standing, standing
Standing on the rock that anchors my soul
Standing, standing
Standing on the rock of revelation
Standing, standing
Standing on the rock that will not roll

I'm not alone
He's always beside me
In the midst of the storm
His hand's there to guide me
I will not fear
For He is near

Standing on the rock, standing on the rock
Standing
Standing on the rock, standing on the rock
Standing

Don't Take It For Granted

We must have a revelation of Who God is to worship Him. We have to know Him to worship Him. We don't worship Him because of who we are; we worship Him because of Who He is.

There are a lot of musicians who have no relationship with God. They have a lot of ability, but no knowledge of who God is. You can tell from their lives. You can tell from the words they speak.

They never talk about what God is doing; they always talk about what they are doing. They never talk about what God has accomplished; they always talk about what they have accomplished. They never talk about how great God is; they only talk about how great they are.

That is the difference between a musician and a worshiper.

Don't ever fall into the trap of saying, "I'm so talented that everyone should appreciate me just because of how good I am." Talent and ability can end in the blink of an eye or the snap of your fingers.

The young woman who hit Clint head–on did not know that would be the last day she would be able to use anything she had learned at Bible school.

Clint Brown did not know when he was getting dressed that day that it could be the last day he would ever use what God had given him.

He could have died that day. He could have been paralyzed from the waist down. He hit the steering wheel with such impact that his vocal cords could have been permanently damaged. His family's income — his whole lifestyle — depends on his ability to do what he does.

If everything Clint had depended on had been taken from him, where would he be? What was really valuable in his life — his relationship with God — became explicitly clear during this tragic situation.

When we minister on a platform before God's people, it's not just because of our ability. It is because God has called us and equipped us to do what we are doing.

It is easy to begin to take it for granted. We can become accustomed to it, until it becomes common . . . and it loses its value.

The book of Daniel records a story of what happened to a man named Belshazzar when he considered the things of God common.

Belshazzar was the king of the great Babylonian empire. He gave a great feast for a thousand of his lords. When they had begun to drink their wine, he called for the golden vessels that his grandfather Nebuchadnezzar had taken from the Temple of God at Jerusalem.

He appropriated these vessels, which had been sanctified for the worship of God, and gave them to his guests to use to drink their wine and to praise their gods of gold and silver, wood and stone.

In the midst of their reveling, a man's hand appeared and spelled out Belshazzar's doom. *The handwriting was on the wall!*

Belshazzar had been weighed in the balance and found wanting. He had used the holy things of God for a common and unclean purpose. For that reason, his kingdom was finished. The kingdom would be divided and given over to the Medes and the Persians.

The calling of God is a holy thing. Don't ever take the gifts and abilities given to us by God for granted. They are not to be used to satisfy our own desires.

How valuable is what we have on the inside of us? Is our relationship with God the most precious thing we have?

We must never take the things of God for granted. We must become vessels of worship to God every day. Then, when we step onto a platform and break open that vessel, only the pure, holy, undefiled oil of worship will flow out.

What is on the inside will have been guarded and protected against what is on the outside — " . . . **sealed with that holy Spirit of promise**" (Eph. 1:13).

Brother Clint told me of an illustration he used one time at a convention of music directors. It seemed to him that all they could talk about was how wonderful they were, how great their programs were, and how many songs they had published.

He brought a five gallon bucket of water to the platform. He said, "This bucket represents the kingdom of God."

He plunged his arm into the water and said, "My arm represents you and me."

"Where are we?" he asked.

"In the kingdom of God," they answered.

He pulled his arm out, looked at the water, and said, "Now this is the kingdom of God without us. What did it lose? Where's the hole?"

There was no hole! The water completely filled the space his arm had taken up.

"That's how fast God can replace you," he said.

Our relationship with God — the life of God we have on the inside of us — is the most valuable thing we have. God is going to have a people who will worship Him because they know Him.

He will replace those who are in it to serve themselves, and He will put in those who are in it to serve Him.

God knows what we can do and what we cannot do. He knows what His plan is for us.

I know many talented musicians who are not doing anything for God because they are constantly trying to prove how wonderful they are. What God is looking for is a people who will worship Him and make themselves available to be used by Him.

If we look to man to promote us, God never will. If we look to God to promote us, man has no choice.

We are valuable to God. We are designed to be vessels of honor, set apart for the Master's use. When we start pouring out what we are on people, it makes an impact on their lives.

We can be dead water or we can be living water. We can be water that is stagnant or water that is as fresh as a waterfall from heaven. *The choice is ours!*

Fresh Oil

Fresh oil from heaven
Flow with Your power
As we stand in reverence
Fill our hearts

5

Corporate Praise and Worship

The church is returning to an understanding of the reality of praise and worship and to an atmosphere of expectancy. This fresh understanding is producing victory in the lives of believers.

The Spirit of God is being displayed in a new measure, and He is touching those who are placing themselves in such an atmosphere of praise and worship. God is moving in their lives.

Unity Is Costly

"And when the day of Pentecost was fully come, they were all with one accord in one place. And suddenly there came a sound from heaven as of a rushing mighty wind, and it filled all the house where they were sitting. And there appeared unto them cloven tongues like as of fire, and it sat upon each of them. And they were all filled with the Holy Ghost, and began to speak with other tongues, as the Spirit gave them utterance."

Acts 2:1–4

On the day of Pentecost, the 120 were gathered together in one accord in the Upper Room. They were obeying the instructions that Jesus had given them — waiting for an enduement of power from on high. It was surely coming.

Many times, we are waiting for God to do something for us. But the promises of God are already accomplished facts. What remains is for us to place ourselves in a position to receive by getting into agreement with God's Word and with each other.

Results come when there is unity of heart and purpose. Surely the heart of God must be grieved when He looks over His people as they gather together to worship Him, and He sees only halfhearted participation . . . and those who are involved are not even flowing together.

The Psalmist David expresses the heart of God in Psalm 133:1–2,

"Behold, how good and how pleasant it is for brethren to dwell together in unity! It is like the precious ointment upon the head, that ran down upon the beard, even Aaron's beard: that went down to the skirts of his garments."

Unity is costly, but it produces results. The price of unity is the willingness to lay aside our own plans and purposes and adopt God's plans and purposes. It is submitting ourselves to leadership, being willing to follow their instructions and not our own ideas. It is not always easy, and it sometimes hurts.

Think about what would happen on a family vacation without agreement. Suppose Dad said, "We just can't decide where to go on vacation. So here is what we are going to do. Everyone is going to get a turn to drive. You can go wherever you want — north, south, east or west — it doesn't matter."

Dad might start out for the Rocky Mountains. He might drive as far as Chicago before it was Mom's turn to choose. Mom might make a beeline for Saks Fifth Avenue in New York, until Little Brother took the wheel.

Little Brother might take off for Disney World, until Big Sister decides to head for Malibu Beach. Where would they end up? Would they ever get anywhere? Would they ever experience the benefits of being on vacation?

Someone needs to make a decision!

Sometimes a praise service is like that vacation. The worship leader might stand up and say, "Let's lift our voices

72

now in one accord to the Lord. Let's shout unto God with a mighty voice of thanksgiving."

A survey of the congregation right then might show some people clapping, some lifting their hands, some dancing. While all these forms of praise are good, the direction given was to shout. When instructions like this are not followed in a service, it's like the change of route on that vacation. No one can experience the benefits.

Isaiah says, **"All we like sheep have gone astray; we have turned every one to his own way . . ."** (Isa. 53:6).

It's no wonder that God's people are called sheep!

The result is chaos in the realm of the Spirit. When the ranks are broken, the power of God cannot be displayed in full measure. Without unity and obedience, the body cannot be blessed.

The obedience of those who are following instructions can be obscured by the clamor of those following their own dictates. God sees the hearts of the obedient and can bless them individually, but the power of the corporate anointing is lost.

Lord, I Want To Know You

Lord, I want to know You
In the fullness of Who You are
I will push my flesh to the side
To get to where You are
Man's revelation can only take me just so far
Lord, I want to know You for Who You are

The Church Is a Body

When we come together in unity to praise and worship God, it is a pleasing demonstration to Him of the body of Christ.

73

The Apostle Paul describes this body in 1 Corinthians 12:

"For as the body is one, and hath many members, and all the members of that one body, being many, are one body: so also is Christ ['s body].

"For the body is not one member, but many.

"And the eye cannot say unto the hand, I have no need of thee: nor again the head to the feet, I have no need of you.

"Nay, much more those members of the body, which seem to be more feeble, are necessary:

"And whether one member suffer, all the members suffer with it; or one member be honoured, all the members rejoice with it.

"Now ye are the body of Christ, and members in particular."

vv. 12,14,21,22,26,27

The hand cannot make decisions apart from the foot. Can the hand go one place and the foot another? It is necessary for all the parts of the body to work together to accomplish a goal.

"Take all the men of war, and march around Jericho — once a day for six days," God told Joshua. "On the seventh day, march around seven times, let the priests blow the trumpets and let all the people shout."

They did as Joshua instructed. They marched around and began to lift up their praise, and the Bible says that the walls came down. (Josh. 6.) Through obedience, and through uniting together, they obtained the victory.

It's time to become one body, lifting up the praises of God together. What each member does affects everyone else. Obedience or disobedience will affect the course of a service and the manifestation of God in our midst.

Unity is costly, but it produces victory.

The church is realizing the importance of praise. The church is realizing the power of unity. The church is realizing that God is sovereign, and that God has a plan.

We Glorify Your Name
We glorify Your Name
You're forever more the same
We bring honor and thanksgiving
And worship You with praise

We will lift our voice
In You we will rejoice
You are holy and we glorify
Holy and we glorify
Holy and we glorify Your Name

Coals of Fire

I have the greatest parents in the world. I have seen the character of my heavenly Father reflected in my natural father. We can learn a lot by observing the spiritual principles in natural things.

My father has always loved a good fire. He prides himself on keeping a fire going. As a child, I remember him banking the fire every night before we went to bed.

He would scoop out the day's ashes and pack them down over the embers of the fire.

I would ask him, "Daddy, why are you doing that? Why are you covering up the fire?"

"Well, son," he would say, "I'm just preserving it. I'll just stir it up in the morning, and we'll have a good fire again."

In the morning, I would find my dad down on his knees in front of that heap of gray ash.

"Where's the fire, Daddy?" I would ask.

"You just watch, son, and you'll see."

I would watch him begin to blow away the ash until the embers were exposed. He would fan those embers until the flames were rekindled.

Now the world might think that the church has been lulled to sleep, but I have some news for them: God's breath is blowing on the church today.

Underneath the ashes of yesterday's fire are the red hot coals of revival!

The prophet Ezekiel had a vision of a man clothed in linen, with a writer's ink horn in his hand. God sent the man through the city of Jerusalem to mark those who cried out against the sin and abomination there. Those who remained unmarked were to be slain utterly. (Ezek. 9.) Ezekiel feared that "all the residue of Israel" would be destroyed.

But God had other plans . . .

"Go in, . . ." He told the man in linen, "and fill thine hand with coals of fire from between the cherubims, and scatter them over the city" (Ezek. 10:2).

The man went in and did as God commanded.

The world might look at the church and think that sin has utterly destroyed it. But God has a remnant — coals of fire from the altar — being scattered throughout the world today.

The church is not dead. The church is not asleep. There is a remnant generation banked under the ashes of defeat, ready to burst into the greatest revival fire the world has ever seen!

There is a remnant generation reaching for a new day.

Pursue Praise

Pursuit is the proof of desire. The evidence that we want victory is our pursuit of praise. To obtain something, we must pursue something.

A friend of Clint's who played high school football received an invitation from his hometown university to visit a football game and view college life.

During the course of his classroom observations, he came upon a group of senior students displaying unruly behavior — horsing around in class, throwing spitballs, laughing and joking, not paying attention.

He overheard the aged professor making his final comments to the class. He wasn't congratulating them on their fine achievements or their valuable investment in higher education. Rather, he looked at them through the eyes of someone who has been there and said, "My greatest fear today is that you are going to accomplish exactly what you have pursued for the last four years."

At first, the young man did not understand the professor's comment. Why would the professor fear for what they would achieve?

But as he gave it thought, he realized that if their behavior was any indication of their lifestyle, they had probably not pursued anything!

They were about to reap exactly what they had sown.

Our willingness to pursue praise by praising God for the victory before we see it shows God our faith. Faith — our pursuit of praise — gives God the opportunity to go to work on our behalf. When we come together with one heart and one mind, no force of the enemy will be able to stand in our way.

Soldiers of Light
We come against the powers of darkness
We stand with strength and hold up the light
His Word illuminates our path
as we go forward
For it's by faith we walk and not by sight

Like the noise of chariots on the mountain
Like the sound of a mighty rushing wind

Like the flame of a fire
that devours our enemy

When the soldiers of light appear
All darkness must flee

The Battle Is the Lord's

Praise lays the foundation for victory. In Psalm 100:4, David instructs, **"Enter into his gates with thanksgiving, and into his courts with praise: be thankful unto him, and bless his name."**

A service without thanksgiving and praise will be void of power. Thanksgiving and praise precede every battle of life. Praising God before the battle begins assures us of the victory.

In 2 Chronicles 20, the children of Ammon and Moab came against Jehoshaphat, king of Judah, to destroy him. The prophetic voice of God came to Jehoshaphat through a young man named Jahaziel:

> **"Thus saith the Lord unto you, Be not afraid nor dismayed by reason of this great multitude; for the battle is not yours, but God's. Tomorrow go ye down against them . . . Ye shall not need to fight in this battle: set yourselves, stand ye still, and see the salvation of the Lord with you, O Judah and Jerusalem: fear not, nor be dismayed; tomorrow go out against them: for the Lord will be with you."**

vv. 15–17

Jehoshaphat could have said, "Now, wait a minute. Not only are the people of Moab coming after me, but Ammon's coming after me, too. I'm outnumbered! And who is this young upstart anyway, saying, 'Thus saith the Lord'?"

But he did not react that way. Instead, Jehoshaphat took the people toward the battle, praising God with a loud voice.

"Believe in the Lord your God, so shall ye be established," Jehoshaphat told them. "Believe his prophets, so shall ye prosper." And he appointed singers to go before the army, saying, "Praise the Lord; for his mercy endureth for ever" (vv. 20,21).

"And when they began to sing and to praise, the Lord set ambushments against the children of Ammon, Moab, and mount Seir . . . utterly to slay and destroy them. . . ."

vv. 22–23

What kind of God would say, "Lay down your sword and pick up a trumpet" in the time of battle? What kind of God would say, "Lay down your shield and pick up a tambourine" in the time of war?

There is another lesson in this story. Not only will the battle be fought and won through praise, but many times the destruction of the enemy becomes the answer to a need.

"And when Jehoshaphat and his people came to take away the spoil of them, they found among them in abundance both riches with the dead bodies, and precious jewels, which they stripped off for themselves, more than they could carry away: and they were three days in gathering of the spoil, it was so much."

v. 25

The battles recorded in the Word of God were always preceded by praise. At the end of the battle, the children of Israel offered praise and thanksgiving for the victory. There were times they did not win their battles; but through the battles, the Israelites learned. They always gave thanks for the victory.

The victory Jehoshaphat won was the result of praise. After the Lord set the ambushments against their enemies and destroyed them, they assembled themselves together and blessed the Lord, singing and praising God with psalteries and harps and trumpets.

And the Bible says **"the realm of Jehoshaphat was quiet: for his God gave him rest round about"** (v. 30).

Through their praise, God defeated their enemies, provided for their material needs, and gave them peace. This was the kind of God they served.

Theirs was a God who was vitally interested in every aspect of their lives. Theirs was a God whose plan for them was complete and total victory . . . a God whose plan for them was to praise and worship Him. And this God is still God today!

Going Forth Into Battle

We're going forth into battle
With praise as a weapon of war
Slaying all of our enemies
Claiming all of their spoils
We're going forth into battle
With songs of victory
Binding up the strong man
Setting the captives free

Our God is a God of vengeance
Making war with our praise
We're going to win 'cause we're making war
With one voice His power's extended
As we magnify His Name

I refuse to be refused
I deny to be denied
Satan, we're coming after you
We're going to stand our ground
And take back what is ours

6

Leadership Keys

God has a specific goal and purpose for each local body. The methods may differ, but the principles are the same — truth is universal.

We are often asked questions about our praise and worship program at World Harvest Church. We trust that the answers you find here will help you carry out God's plan for your ministry.

Q. I hear you talk a lot about vision. Will you explain the importance of vision?

A. Vision simply means the plans and purposes of God for your local body. The prophet Habakkuk says, **"Write the vision, and make it plain"** (Hab. 2:2). Understanding the vision of God for your local church is fundamental to promoting an atmosphere of praise and worship. If we don't have a clear idea of what God has directed us to do, how can we expect people to rally around us and support our cause?

We must take the time to impart the vision into the hearts and lives of the people we work with, **"that he may run that readeth it."** As leaders, we must take every opportunity — and make opportunities — to put what is inside of us into them.

We give each member of our praise and worship team a printed copy of the vision for the music program. We also plan activities and times of teaching to make these concepts alive and practical for them.

Q. How do you get people to be faithful to their commitment to participate in a praise and worship team?

A. One of the most important areas to address in a candidate for the praise and worship team is the area of faithfulness and commitment.

It is important to look at a person's commitment level before giving them a position of responsibility. By doing so, a lot of problems can be avoided before they start.

Dependability and dedication are more valuable than talent. You can take a person who is dependable and dedicated and better their gift. You can often learn a lot about a person just by listening to them talk. A person whose heart is in what he is doing will stay with you.

Q. How do you select the people who are a part of your praise and worship team?

A. We have tryouts periodically for both band and choir.

With any group of people, there must always be a clear understanding of authority. The first question people ask is, "Who's in charge?"

Sometimes it is hard for a person to submit to the authority of a leader, especially if that person is talented or skilled. The world has told them to "look out for number one" and to "do your own thing." Why shouldn't they be in charge — after all, they are so talented, you see.

Understanding that God's authority rests in appointment makes this a simple matter. We don't submit to someone because they are highly skilled or always right; we submit because they have been placed in authority over us by God.

"And we beseech you, brethren, to know them which labour among you, and are over you in the Lord, and admonish you; And to esteem them very highly in love for their work's sake. And be at peace among yourselves."

1 Thessalonians 5:12–13

When there is unity and peace, you have set the stage for the anointing of God to flow.

In 1 Timothy 3:6, Paul warns us not to place a novice in a position of responsibility in the church. I personally review all candidates, along with Clint Brown and a member of my ministry staff. We review membership files, and we get feedback from current areas of involvement in the church. Everyone must be a member in good standing of World Harvest Church and must complete the Firm Foundations membership course.

We listen to a person's vocal quality and ability to harmonize. We also like a person to have a neat and pleasant appearance.

Q. You seem to have so many people who are very talented. How important is it to have talented people to use for praise and worship?

A. When considering a person for a position of service, talent should not be the sole consideration. Especially in those times when you really need someone to fill a certain role, it's much better to wait than to make a wrong decision. Trust God to send the people you need.

Talent won't carry a person the distance. People with ability will come and go, but only those with faithfulness and dedication will stay. How many times have we seen a talented person placed in a visible role (like the music ministry) excel and then fall away? The acclaim, the applause, and the recognition often prove to be too much. Without the development of character along with the development of talent, you will soon be dealing with a problem.

Samuel the prophet was sent to Bethlehem to anoint a king from among Jesse's sons. As each son passed by Samuel, God said something very interesting.

"Look not on his countenance, or on the height of his stature; because I have refused him: for the Lord seeth not as man seeth; for man looketh on the outward appearance, but the Lord looketh on the heart."

1 Samuel 16:7

God's choice was David, whom the Bible calls a man after God's own heart. Pray, and God will give you direction about who to use.

This must be balanced with the fact that you do need people with a certain amount of ability. Any time you begin to build something, it's wise to surround yourself with people who know more than you do! A good support team will help you develop and will provide a solid foundation for praise and worship in the church.

Q. How does the music team prepare for services?

A. Clint has a weekly practice, one evening a week, with the entire praise and worship team. They meet together in the sanctuary. The first order of business is to exercise — by walking twice around the concourse of the church!

Our arranger then takes the band into a separate room to rehearse, while the choir and singers learn their parts. After about an hour, they come back into the sanctuary and put both parts together. Clint usually teaches them one or two new songs every week.

One advantage we have is that most of our rhythm section and front line singers work at the church, so day time practices are easier for Clint to arrange. Without this, we would have to schedule another evening practice, which is difficult for most people.

The band and choir meet an hour before each service on Sunday for a sound check. After that, there is time for personal Bible reading and prayer. We also pray corporately before each service begins.

The most important preparation is what each individual does before coming to church. We encourage them to take some extra time on Saturday night to pray and prepare for the service.

Q. Do you think it is a good idea to have a song list prepared?

A. Yes, it is a good idea — for several reasons. A numbered list allows you the flexibility to change songs easily. All Clint needs to do is to relay the number instead of trying to make himself understood saying the name of the song.

When you have a list that you have prayed about, you can go with it confidently if nothing else seems to be happening.

A list can be restrictive if you always follow it song by song. Always allow yourself the freedom to change songs as you feel the Spirit directing you.

Q. How does a praise and worship team learn to flow with you in anointing?

A. They learn by doing it. Always pay attention to what is happening in the service. Watch what works, what doesn't, and why. Think ahead.

I give our praise and worship team the opportunity to learn from their mistakes. I will let them go on, even if what we are doing isn't working, so they can learn how to recover it.

I encourage them to study my books and tapes so they are familiar with the messages I am currently preaching; this way they will understand the flow of God we are in.

We strive to be sensitive to the leading of the Spirit of God and not to hesitate to go with what we feel God wants us to do. When we take that step of faith out into uncharted waters, God meets us there.

Q. How do you decide which songs to use in your services?

A. Most of the songs we sing have been written by Clint Brown, or one of our assistant music directors. We are always listening to new music, looking for songs that we can use.

It is important that the music you use reflects the message your pastor preaches. That is why we write most of our own music. Music is a powerful vehicle to use to take a pastor's messages and put them into the hearts of the people.

Every part of a ministry should reflect and support the overall vision, and music is no exception.

Q. How long do you think the praise and worship part of the service should be?

A. First of all, praise and worship isn't "part" of the service — it is the service. We come to church to praise and worship God. Every aspect of the service is directed that way — the music, the giving, the preaching.

In our services, the praise and worship team ministers in music until I make a change in the order of the service. If I decide not to change the direction, they are prepared to minister themselves the entire service!

Q. We have just started a church. What can we do if we do not have any musicians yet?

A. I have heard reports of churches using our music tapes or service videos to have church. This idea can work, but you have to guard against being locked in. But what do you do if you want to change in a way your tape doesn't? You have to make a choice at this point. You can try to change tapes or you can go on and sing without music.

The best — and most important — thing you can do is to begin to pray for God to send in the people you need. Begin to pray, and watch what God will do for you!

Q. How do you bring people into the presence of God?

A. The most effective way to draw people into the presence of God is to be there yourself. As a leader, you should already have been before God before you ever step foot on a platform.

Anything that says, "You must use me to get to God" is a religious act. When we begin to say, "This is what it takes to get into the presence of God," we are becoming religious. We know that it is relationship, not religion, that allows us into the presence of God.

Relationship — knowing God, and knowing His voice — will allow you to follow the leading of the Spirit and to know how to lead the people every service.

Q. Sometimes it's hard to get our congregation actively involved in praise and worship. How do you teach people to praise and worship?

A. You teach them by your example. Your congregation will go no further than you do. If you are free, they will become free. Often, all people need is an example to follow. You can expect no more of them than you expect of yourself.

When my congregation sees me rejoicing, they will rejoice. When they see me dancing and lifting my hands, they will dance and lift their hands.

It is important to begin to instill a love for praise and worship into the children in your congregation. If you want tomorrow's adults to be free, you must begin with today's children.

Children love to participate in the songs they sing. Be creative and give them lots of interaction — sound effects, special ways to clap, certain times to jump or spin or yell, surprise endings. It will hold their interest and let them know that you really care about their praise and worship.

Q. Why are you so aggressive about your praise and worship? Aren't you afraid people might criticize you?

A. Jesus came to annihilate the works of the devil. Our purpose is to demonstrate that annihilation. The devil is under our feet. As long as he's there, let's just dance on his head awhile!

Jesus, speaking to the church of Laodicea, said He knew their works — He called them lukewarm. He said He would rather that they were hot or cold. (Rev. 3:15–16.)

With the revival fires of God in our hearts, how can we help but praise Him — with our whole heart, and soul, and mind, and strength. *It's like fire shut up in our bones!*

Our God Is a God of Fire

Our God is a God of fire
He sent His Son with one desire
His purpose was to annihilate
He created us to demonstrate
There ain't no doubt
About His power
Yes, our God
Is a God of fire

Igniting me — I'm on fire
Infusing me — I'm on fire
Possessing me with fire

Additional References

Old Testament

Exodus 34:14 For thou shalt worship no other god: for the Lord, whose name is Jealous, is a jealous God.

Joshua 5:14 And he said, Nay; but as captain of the host of the Lord am I now come. And Joshua fell on his face to the earth, and did worship, and said unto him, What saith my lord unto his servant?

Judges 5:1 Then sang Deborah and Barak the son of Abinoam on that day.

Judges 5:3 Hear, O ye kings; give ear, O ye princes; I, even I, will sing unto the Lord; I will sing praise to the Lord God of Israel.

1 Samuel 2:1 And Hannah prayed, and said, My heart rejoiceth in the Lord, mine horn is exalted in the Lord: my mouth is enlarged over mine enemies; because I rejoice in thy salvation.

2 Samuel 7:26 And let thy name be magnified for ever, saying, The Lord of hosts is the God over Israel: and let the house of thy servant David be established before thee.

2 Samuel 22:47 The Lord liveth; and blessed be my rock; and exalted be the God of the rock of my salvation.

2 King 17:36 But the Lord, who brought you up out of the land of Egypt with great power and a stretched out arm, him shall ye fear, and him shall ye worship, and to him shall ye do sacrifice.

1 Chronicles 16:8 Give thanks unto the Lord, call upon his name, make known his deeds among the people.

v. 9 Sing unto him, sing psalms unto him, talk ye of all his won-drous works.

v. 10 Glory ye in his holy name: let the heart of them rejoice that seek the Lord.

1 Chronicles 16:24 Declare his glory among the heathen; his marvellous works among all nations.

v. 25 For great is the Lord, and greatly to be praised: he also is to be feared above all gods.

1 Chronicles 16:29 Give unto the Lord the glory due unto his name: bring an offering, and come before him: worship the Lord in the beauty of holiness.

1 Chronicles 16:34 O give thanks unto the Lord; for he is good; for his mercy endureth for ever.

1 Chronicles 23:5 Moreover four thousand were porters; and four thousand praised the Lord with the instruments which I made, said David, to praise therewith.

1 Chronicles 29:11 Thine, O Lord, is the greatness, and the power, and the glory, and the victory, and the majesty: for all that is in the heaven and in the earth is thine; thine is the kingdom, O Lord, and thou art exalted as head above all.

1 Chronicles 29:13 Now therefore, our God, we thank thee, and praise thy glorious name.

2 Chronicles 5:12 Also the Levites which were the singers, all of them of Asaph, of Heman, of Jeduthun, with their sons and their brethren, being arrayed in white linen, having cymbals and psalteries and harps, stood at the east end of the altar, and with them an hundred and twenty priests sounding with trumpets.

2 Chronicles 20:21 And when he had consulted with the people, he appointed singers unto the Lord, and that should praise the beauty of holiness, as they went out before the army, and to say, Praise the Lord; for his mercy endureth for ever.

v. 22 And when they began to sing and to praise, the Lord set ambushments against the children of Ammon, Moab, and mount Seir, which were come against Judah; and they were smitten.

2 Chronicles 23:13 And she looked, and, behold, the king stood at his pillar at the entering in, and the princes and the trumpets by the king: and all the people of the land rejoiced, and sounded with trumpets, also the singers with instruments of musick, and such as taught to sing praise. Then Athaliah rent her clothes, and said, Treason, Treason.

Job 21:12 They take the timbrel and harp, and rejoice at the sound of the organ.

Psalm 5:7 But as for me, I will come into thy house in the multitude of thy mercy: and in thy fear will I worship toward thy holy temple.

Psalm 7:17 I will praise the Lord according to his righteousness: and will sing praise to the name of the Lord most high.

Psalm 9:1 I will praise thee, O Lord, with my whole heart; I will shew forth all thy marvellous works.

v. 2 I will be glad and rejoice in thee: I will sing praise to thy name, O thou most High.

Psalm 9:14 That I may shew forth all thy praise in the gates of the daughter of Zion: I will rejoice in thy salvation.

Psalm 18:46 The Lord liveth; and blessed be my rock; and let the God of my salvation be exalted.

Psalm 18:49 Therefore will I give thanks unto thee, O Lord, among the heathen, and sing praises unto thy name.

Psalm 21:13 Be thou exalted, Lord, in thine own strength: so will we sing and praise thy power.

Psalm 22:22 I will declare thy name unto my brethren: in the midst of the congregation will I praise thee.

v. 23 Ye that fear the Lord, praise him; all ye the seed of Jacob, glorify him; and fear him, all ye the seed of Israel.

v. 24 For he hath not despised nor abhorred the affliction of the afflicted; neither hath he hid his face from him; but when he cried unto him, he heard.

v. 25 My praise shall be of thee in the great congregation: I will pay my vows before them that fear him.

v. 26 The meek shall eat and be satisfied: they shall praise the Lord that seek him: your heart shall live for ever.

v. 27 All the ends of the world shall remember and turn unto the Lord: and all the kindreds of the nations shall worship before thee.

v. 28 For the kingdom is the Lord's: and he is the governor among the nations.

v. 29 All they that be fat upon earth shall eat and worship: all they that go down to the dust shall bow before him: and none can keep alive his own soul.

Psalm 27:6 And now shall mine head be lifted up above mine enemies round about me: therefore will I offer in his tabernacle sacrifices of joy; I will sing, yea, I will sing praises unto the Lord.

Psalm 28:7 The Lord is my strength and my shield; my heart trusted in him, and I am helped: therefore my heart greatly rejoiceth; and with my song will I praise him.

Psalm 29:2 Give unto the Lord the glory due unto his name; worship the Lord in the beauty of holiness.

Psalm 30:11 Thou hast turned for me my mourning into dancing: thou hast put off my sackcloth, and girded me with gladness;

v. 12 To the end that my glory may sing praise to thee, and not be silent. O Lord my God, I will give thanks unto thee for ever.

Psalm 32:11 Be glad in the Lord, and rejoice ye righteous: and shout for joy, all ye that are upright in heart.

Psalm 33:1 Rejoice in the Lord, O ye righteous: for praise is comely for the upright.

v. 2 Praise the Lord with harp: sing unto him with the psaltery and an instrument of ten strings.

v. 3 Sing unto him a new song; play skilfully with a loud noise.

v. 4 For the word of the Lord is right; and all his works are done in truth.

Psalm 34:1 I will bless the Lord at all times: his praise shall continually be in my mouth.

v. 2 My soul shall make her boast in the Lord: the humble shall hear thereof, and be glad.

v. 3 O magnify the Lord with me, and let us exalt his name together.

Psalm 35:18 I will give thee thanks in the great congregation: I will praise thee among much people.

Psalm 35:27 Let them shout for joy, and be glad, that favour my righteous cause: yea, let them say continually, Let the Lord be magnified, which hath pleasure in the prosperity of his servant.

Psalm 35:28 And my tongue shall speak of thy righteousness and of thy praise all the day long.

Psalm 40:3 And he hath put a new song in my mouth, even praise unto our God: many shall see it, and fear, and shall trust in the Lord.

Psalm 40:16 Let all those that seek thee rejoice and be glad in thee: let such as love thy salvation say continually, The Lord be magnified.

Psalm 43:4 Then will I go unto the altar of God, unto God my exceeding joy: yea, upon the harp will I praise thee, O God my God.

v. 5 Why art thou cast down, O my soul? and why art thou disquieted within me? hope in God: for I shall yet praise him, who is the health of my countenance, and my God.

Psalm 48:1 Great is the Lord, and greatly to be praised in the city of our God, in the mountain of his holiness.

Psalm 50:23 Whoso offereth praise glorifieth me: and to him that ordereth his conversation aright will I shew the salvation of God.

Psalm 54:6 I will freely sacrifice unto thee: I will praise thy name, O Lord; for it is good.

Psalm 56:10 In God will I praise his word: in the Lord will I praise his word.

v. 11 In God have I put my trust: I will not be afraid what man can do unto me.

v. 12 Thy vows are upon me, O God: I will render praises unto thee.

Psalm 57:5 Be thou exalted, O God, above the heavens; let thy glory be above all the earth.

Psalm 57:7 My heart is fixed, O God, my heart is fixed: I will sing and give praise.

Psalm 57:9 I will praise thee, O Lord, among the people: I will sing unto thee among the nations.

Psalm 63:1 O God, thou art my God; early will I seek thee: my soul thirsteth for thee, my flesh longeth for thee in a dry and thirsty land, where no water is;

v. 2 To see thy power and thy glory, so as I have seen thee in the sanctuary.

v. 3 Because thy lovingkindness is better than life, my lips shall praise thee.

v. 4 Thus will I bless thee while I live: I will lift up my hands in thy name.

v. 5 My soul shall be satisfied as with marrow and fatness; and my mouth shall praise thee with joyful lips:

v. 6 When I remember thee upon my bed, and meditate on thee in the night watches.

v. 7 Because thou hast been my help, therefore in the shadow of thy wings will I rejoice.

Psalm 66:1 Make a joyful noise unto God, all ye lands:

v. 2 Sing forth the honour of his name: make his praise glorious.

v. 3 Say unto God, How terrible art thou in thy works! through the greatness of thy power shall thine enemies submit themselves unto thee.

v. 4 All the earth shall worship thee, and shall sing unto thee; they shall sing to thy name. Selah.

v. 5 Come and see the works of God: he is terrible in his doing toward the children of men.

v. 6 He turned the sea into dry land: they went through the flood on foot: there did we rejoice in him.

v. 7 He ruleth by his power for ever; his eyes behold the nations: let not the rebellious exalt themselves. Selah.

v. 8 O bless our God, ye people, and make the voice of his praise to be heard.

Psalm 67:3 Let the people praise thee, O God; let all the people praise thee.

Psalm 67:5 Let the people praise thee, O God; let all the people praise thee.

Psalm 68:3 But let the righteous be glad; let them rejoice before God: yea, let them exceedingly rejoice.

v. 4 Sing unto God, sing praises to his name: extol him that rideth upon the heavens by his name Jah, and rejoice before him.

Psalm 69:30 I will praise the name of God with a song, and will magnify him with thanksgiving.

v. 31 This also shall please the Lord better than an ox or bullock that hath horns and hoofs.

v. 32 The humble shall see this, and be glad: and your heart shall live that seek God.

v. 33 For the Lord heareth the poor, and despiseth not his prisoners.

v. 34 Let the heaven and earth praise him, the seas, and every thing that moveth therein.

Psalm 70:4 Let all those that seek thee rejoice and be glad in thee: and let such as love thy salvation say continually, Let God be magnified.

Psalm 71:8 Let my mouth be filled with thy praise and with thy honour all the day.

Psalm 71:14 But I will hope continually, and will yet praise thee more and more.

Psalm 71:22 I will also praise thee with the psaltery, even thy truth, O my God: unto thee will I sing with the harp, O thou Holy One of Israel.

Psalm 81:1 Sing aloud unto God our strength: make a joyful noise unto the God of Jacob.

Psalm 86:12 I will praise thee, O Lord my God, with all my heart: and I will glorify thy name for evermore.

Psalm 89:5 And the heavens shall praise thy wonders, O Lord: thy faithfulness also in the congregation of the saints.

Psalm 89:16 In thy name shall they rejoice all the day: and in thy righteousness shall they be exalted.

Psalm 92:1 It is a good thing to give thanks unto the Lord, and to sing praises unto thy name, O most High:

v. 2 To shew forth thy lovingkindness in the morning, and thy faithfulness every night,

v. 3 Upon an instrument of ten strings, and upon the psaltery; upon the harp with a solemn sound.

Psalm 95:1 O come, let us sing unto the Lord: let us make a joyful noise to the rock of our salvation.

v. 2 Let us come before his presence with thanksgiving, and make a joyful noise unto him with psalms.

v. 3 For the Lord is a great God, and a great King above all gods.

v. 4 In his hand are the deep places of the earth: the strength of the hills is his also.

v. 5 The sea is his, and he made it: and his hands formed the dry land.

v. 6 O come, let us worship and bow down: let us kneel before the Lord our maker.

v. 7 For he is our God; and we are the people of his pasture, and the sheep of his hand. . . .

Psalm 96:1 O sing unto the Lord a new song: sing unto the Lord, all the earth.

v. 2 Sing unto the Lord, bless his name; shew forth his salvation from day to day.

v. 3 Declare his glory among the heathen, his wonders among all people.

v. 4 For the Lord is great, and greatly to be praised: he is to be feared above all gods.

v. 5 For all the gods of the nations are idols: but the Lord made the heavens.

v. 6 Honour and majesty are before him: strength and beauty are in his sanctuary.

v. 7 Give unto the Lord, O ye kindreds of the people, give unto the Lord glory and strength.

v. 8 Give unto the Lord the glory due unto his name: bring an offering, and come into his courts.

v. 9 O worship the Lord in the beauty of holiness: fear before him, all the earth.

v. 10 Say among the heathen that the Lord reigneth: the world also shall be established that is shall not be moved: he shall judge the people righteously.

v. 11 Let the heavens rejoice, and let the earth be glad; let the sea roar, and the fulness thereof.

v. 12 Let the field be joyful, and all that is therein: then shall all the trees of the wood rejoice

v. 13 Before the Lord: for he cometh, for he cometh to judge the earth: he shall judge the world with righteousness, and the people with his truth.

Psalm 97:9 For thou, Lord, art high above all the earth: thou art exalted far above all gods.

Psalm 98:1 O sing unto the Lord a new song; for he hath done marvellous things: his right hand, and his holy arm, hath gotten him the victory.

v. 2 The Lord hath made known his salvation: his righteousness hath he openly shewed in the sight of the heathen.

v. 3 He hath remembered his mercy and his truth toward the house of Israel: all the ends of the earth have seen the salvation of our God.

v. 4 Make a joyful noise unto the Lord, all the earth: make a loud noise, and rejoice, and sing praise.

v. 5 Sing unto the Lord with the harp; with the harp, and the voice of a psalm.

v. 6 With trumpets and sound of cornet make a joyful noise before the Lord, the King.

Psalm 99:3 Let them praise thy great and terrible name; for it is holy.

Psalm 99:5 Exalt ye the Lord our God, and worship at his footstool; for he is holy.

Psalm 99:9 Exalt the Lord our God, and worship at his holy hill; for the Lord our God is holy.

Psalm 100:1 Make a joyful noise unto the Lord, all ye lands.

v. 2 Serve the Lord with gladness: come before his presence with singing.

v. 3 Know ye that the Lord he is God: it is he that hath made us, and not we ourselves; we are his people, and the sheep of his pasture.

v. 4 Enter into his gates with thanksgiving, and into his courts with praise: be thankful unto him, and bless his name.

v. 5 For the Lord is good; his mercy is everlasting; and his truth endureth to all generations.

Psalm 104:33 I will sing unto the Lord as long as I live: I will sing praise to my God while I have my being.

Psalm 105:2 Sing unto him, sing psalms unto him: talk ye of all his wondrous works.

Psalm 106:1 Praise ye the Lord. O give thanks unto the Lord; for he is good: for his mercy endureth for ever.

Psalm 106:12 Then believed they his words; they sang his praise.

Psalm 107:8 Oh that men would praise the Lord for his goodness, and for his wonderful works to the children of men!

Psalm 107:32 Let them exalt him also in the congregation of the people, and praise him in the assembly of the elders.

Psalm 108:1 O God, my heart is fixed; I will sing and give praise, even with my glory.

Psalm 108:3 I will praise thee, O Lord, among the people: and I will sing praises unto thee among the nations.

Psalm 109:30 I will greatly praise the Lord with my mouth; yea, I will praise him among the multitude.

Psalm 111:1 Praise ye the Lord. I will praise the Lord with my whole heart, in the assembly of the upright, and in the congregation.

Psalm 112:1 Praise ye the Lord. Blessed is the man that feareth the Lord, that delighteth greatly in his commandments.

Psalm 113:1 Praise ye the Lord. Praise, O ye servants of the Lord, praise the name of the Lord.

Psalm 117:1 O praise the Lord, all ye nations: praise him, all ye people.

v. 2 For his merciful kindness is great toward us: and the truth of the Lord endureth for ever. Praise ye the Lord.

Psalm 118:19 Open to me the gates of righteousness: I will go into them, and I will praise the Lord.

Psalm 118:21 I will praise thee: for thou hast heard me, and art become my salvation.

Psalm 118:28 Thou art my God, and I will praise thee: thou art my God, I will exalt thee.

Psalm 119:7 I will praise thee with uprightness of heart, when I shall have learned thy righteous judgments.

Psalm 119:171 My lips shall utter praise, when thou hast taught me thy statutes.

Psalm 119:175 Let my soul live, and it shall praise thee; and let thy judgments help me.

Psalm 135:1 Praise ye the Lord. Praise ye the name of the Lord; praise him, O ye servants of the Lord.

Psalm 135:3 Praise the Lord; for the Lord is good: sing praises unto his name; for it is pleasant.

Psalm 135:21 Blessed be the Lord out of Zion, which dwelleth at Jerusalem. Praise ye the Lord.

Psalm 138:1 I will praise thee with my whole heart: before the gods will I sing praise unto thee.

v. 2 I will worship toward thy holy temple, and praise thy name for thy lovingkindness and for thy truth: for thou hast magnified thy word above all thy name.

Psalm 138:4 All the kings of the earth shall praise thee, O Lord, when they hear the words of thy mouth.

Psalm 139:14 I will praise thee; for I am fearfully and wonderfully made: marvellous are thy works; and that my soul knoweth right well.

Psalm 144:9 I will sing a new song unto thee, O God: upon a psaltery and an instrument of ten strings will I sing praises unto thee.

Psalm 145:1 I will extol thee, my God, O king; and I will bless thy name for ever and ever.

v. 2 Every day will I bless thee; and I will praise thy name for ever and ever.

v. 3 Great is the Lord, and greatly to be praised; and his greatness is unsearchable.

v. 4 One generation shall praise thy works to another, and shall declare thy mighty acts.

Psalm 145:10 All thy works shall praise thee, O Lord; and thy saints shall bless thee.

Psalm 145:21 My mouth shall speak the praise of the Lord: and let all flesh bless his holy name for ever and ever.

Psalm 146:1 Praise ye the Lord. Praise the Lord, O my soul.

v. 2 While I live will I praise the Lord: I will sing praises unto my God while I have any being.

Psalm 146:10 The Lord shall reign for ever, even thy God, O Zion, unto all generations. Praise ye the Lord.

Psalm 147:1 Praise ye the Lord: for it is good to sing praises unto our God; for it is pleasant; and praise is comely.

Psalm 147:7 Sing unto the Lord with thanksgiving; sing praise upon the harp unto our God.

Psalm 147:12 Praise the Lord, O Jerusalem; praise thy God, O Zion.

Psalm 147:20 He hath not dealt so with any nation: and as for his judgments, they have not known them. Praise ye the Lord.

Psalm 148:1 Praise ye the Lord. Praise ye the Lord from the heavens: praise him in the heights.

v. 2 Praise ye him, all his angels: praise ye him, all his hosts.

v. 3 Praise ye him, sun and moon: praise him, all ye stars of light.

v. 4 Praise him, ye heavens of heavens, and ye waters that be above the heavens.

v. 5 Let them praise the name of the Lord: for he commanded, and they were created.

Psalm 148:13 Let them praise the name of the Lord: for his name alone is excellent; his glory is above the earth and heaven.

v. 14 He also exalteth the horn of his people, the praise of all his saints; even of the children of Israel, a people near unto him. Praise ye the Lord.

Psalm 149:1 Praise ye the Lord. Sing unto the Lord a new song, and his praise in the congregation of saints.

Psalm 149:3 Let them praise his name in the dance: let them sing praises unto him with the timbrel and harp.

Psalm 149:6 Let the high praises of God be in their mouth, and a two–edged sword in their hand.

Psalm 150:1 Praise ye the Lord. Praise God in his sanctuary: praise him in the firmament of his power.

v. 2 Praise him for his mighty acts: praise him according to his excellent greatness.

v. 3 Praise him with the sound of the trumpet: praise him with the psaltery and harp.

v. 4 Praise him with the timbrel and dance: praise him with stringed instruments and organs.

v. 5 Praise him upon the loud cymbals: praise him upon the high sounding cymbals.

v. 6 Let every thing that hath breath praise the Lord. Praise ye the Lord.

Proverb 27:2 Let another man praise thee, and not thine own mouth; a stranger, and not thine own lips.

Proverb 27:21 As the fining pot for silver, and the furnace for gold; so is a man to his praise.

Proverb 28:4 They that forsake the law praise the wicked: but such as keep the law contend with them.

Isaiah 2:2 And it shall come to pass in the last days, that the mountain of the Lord's house shall be established in the top of the mountains, and shall be exalted above the hills; and all nations shall flow unto it.

Isaiah 12:4 And in that day shall ye say, Praise the Lord, call upon his name, declare his doings among the people, make mention that his name is exalted.

Isaiah 13:2 Lift ye up a banner upon the high mountain, exalt the voice unto them, shake the hand, that they may go into the gates of the nobles.

Isaiah 25:1 O Lord, thou art my God; I will exalt thee, I will praise thy name; for thou hast done wonderful things; thy counsels of old are faithfulness and truth.

Isaiah 33:5 The Lord is exalted; for he dwelleth on high: he hath filled Zion with judgment and righteousness.

Isaiah 38:18 For the grave cannot praise thee, death can not celebrate thee: they that go down into the pit cannot hope for thy truth.

v. 19 The living, the living, he shall praise thee, as I do this day: the father to the children shall make known thy truth.

Isaiah 42:8 I am the Lord: that is my name: and my glory will I not give to another, neither my praise to graven images.

Isaiah 42:10 Sing unto the Lord a new song, and his praise from the end of the earth, ye that go down to the sea, and all that is therein; the isles, and the inhabitants thereof.

Isaiah 42:12 Let them give glory unto the Lord, and declare his praise in the islands.

Isaiah 43:21 This people have I formed for myself; they shall shew forth my praise.

Isaiah 61:3 To appoint unto them that mourn in Zion, to give unto them beauty for ashes, the oil of joy for mourning, the garment of praise for the spirit of heaviness; that they might be called trees of righteousness, the planting of the Lord, that he might be glorified.

Isaiah 61:11 For as the earth bringeth forth her bud, and as the garden causeth the things that are sown in it to spring forth; so the Lord God will cause righteousness and praise to spring forth before all the nations.

Jeremiah 17:26 And they shall come from the cities of Judah, and from the places about Jerusalem, and from the land of Benjamin, and from the plain, and from the mountains, and from the south, bringing burnt offerings, and sacrifices, and meat offerings, and incense, and bringing sacrifices of praise, unto the house of the Lord.

Jeremiah 20:13 Sing unto the Lord, praise ye the Lord: for he hath delivered the soul of the poor from the hand of evil-doers.

Jeremiah 26:2 Thus saith the Lord; Stand in the court of the Lord's house, and speak unto all the cities of Judah, which come to worship in the Lord's house, all the words that I command thee to speak unto them; diminish not a word.

Jeremiah 31:7 For thus saith the Lord; Sing with gladness for Jacob, and shout among the chief of the nations: publish ye, praise ye, and say, O Lord, save thy people, the remnant of Israel.

Jeremiah 33:9 And it shall be to me a name of joy, a praise and an honour before all the nations of the earth, which shall hear all the good that I do unto them: and they shall fear and tremble for all the goodness and for all the prosperity that I procure unto it.

Jeremiah 33:11 The voice of joy, and the voice of gladness, the voice of the bridegroom, and the voice of the bride, the voice of them that shall say, Praise the Lord of hosts: for the Lord is good; for his mercy endureth for ever: and of them that shall bring the sacrifice of praise into the house of the Lord. For I will cause to return the captivity of the land, as at the first, saith the Lord.

New Testament

Matthew 15:9 But in vain they do worship me, teaching for doctrines the commandments of men.

Matthew 21:16 And said unto him, Hearest thou what these say? And Jesus saith unto them, Yea; have ye never read, Out of the mouth of babes and sucklings thou hast perfected praise?

Luke 4:8 And Jesus answered and said unto him, Get thee behind me, Satan: for it is written, Thou shalt worship the Lord thy God, and him only shalt thou serve.

Luke 18:43 And immediately he received his sight, and followed him, glorifying God: and all the people, when they saw it, gave praise unto God.

Luke 19:37 And when he was come nigh, even now at the descent of the mount of Olives, the whole multitude of the disciples began to rejoice and praise God with a loud voice for all the mighty works that they had seen.

John 4:24 God is a Spirit: and they that worship him must worship him in spirit and in truth.

Romans 15:11 And again, Praise the Lord, all ye Gentiles; and laud him, all ye people.

1 Corinthians 4:5 Therefore judge nothing before the time, until the Lord come, who both will bring to light the hidden things of darkness, and will make manifest the counsels of the hearts: and then shall every man have praise of God.

Ephesians 1:6 To the praise of the glory of his grace, wherein he hath made us accepted in the beloved.

Ephesians 1:12 That we should be to the praise of his glory, who first trusted in Christ.

Ephesians 1:14 Which is the earnest of our inheritance until the redemption of the purchased possession, unto the praise of his glory.

Ephesians 5:19 Speaking to yourselves in psalms and hymns and spiritual songs, singing and making melody in your heart to the Lord.

Philippians 1:11 Being filled with the fruits of righteousness, which are by Jesus Christ, unto the glory and praise of God.

Philippians 3:3 For we are the circumcision, which worship God in the spirit, and rejoice in Christ Jesus, and have no confidence in the flesh.

Philippians 4:8 Finally, brethren, whatsoever things are true, whatsoever things are honest, whatsoever things are just, whatsoever things are pure, whatsoever things are lovely, whatsoever things are of good report; if there be any virtue, and if there be any praise, think on these things.

Colossians 2:23 Which things have indeed a shew of wisdom in will worship, and humility, and neglecting of the body; not in any honour to the satisfying of the flesh.

Hebrews 1:6 And again, when he bringeth in the firstbegotten into the world, he saith, And let all the angels of God worship him.

Hebrews 2:12 Saying, I will declare thy name unto my brethren, in the midst of the church will I sing praise unto thee.

Hebrews 13:15 By him therefore let us offer the sacrifice of praise to God continually, that is, the fruit of our lips giving thanks to his name.

1 Peter 1:7 That the trial of your faith, being much more precious than of gold that perisheth, though it be tried with fire, might be found unto praise and honour and glory at the appearing of Jesus Christ.

1 Peter 4:11 If any man speak, let him speak as the oracles of God; if any man minister, let him do it as of the ability which God giveth: that God in all things may be glorified through Jesus Christ, to whom be praise and dominion for ever and ever. Amen.

1 Peter 5:6 Humble yourselves therefore under the mighty hand of God, that he may exalt you in due time.

Revelation 5:11 And I beheld, and I heard the voice of many angels round about the throne and the beasts and the elders: and the number of them was ten thousand times ten thousand, and thousands of thousands;

v. 12 Saying with a loud voice, Worthy is the Lamb that was slain to receive power, and riches, and wisdom, and strength, and honour, and glory, and blessing.

v. 13 And every creature which is in heaven, and on the earth, and under the earth, and such as are in the sea, and all that are in them, heard I saying, Blessing, and honour, and glory, and power, be unto him that sitteth upon the throne, and unto the Lamb for ever and ever.

v. 14 And the four beasts said, Amen. And the four and twenty elders fell down and worshipped him that liveth for ever and ever.

Revelation 7:11 And all the angels stood round about the throne, and about the elders and the four beasts, and fell before the throne on their faces, and worshipped God,

v. 12 Saying, Amen: Blessing, and glory, and wisdom, and thanksgiving, and honour, and power, and might, be unto our God for ever and ever. Amen.

Revelation 14:7 Saying with a loud voice, Fear God, and give glory to him; for the hour of his judgment is come: and worship him that made heaven, and earth, and the sea, and the fountains of waters.

Revelation 15:4 Who shall not fear thee, O Lord, and glorify thy name? for thou only art holy: for all nations shall come and worship before thee; for thy judgments are made manifest.

Revelation 19:5 And a voice came out of the throne, saying, Praise our God, all ye his servants, and ye that fear him, both small and great.

My Blessing Upon You

You have come to the kingdom of God for such a time as this. This is your hour. Your day. Your opportunity for divine destiny —to cause the Word of God to be fulfilled and the Scripture to declare, **"These that have turned the world upside down are come hither also"** (Acts 17:6).

So, I bless you now.

I bless you beyond myself.

I bless you beyond the capacity of human limitation.

I dig deep within me to the anointing which resides and abides forever, and I release that anointing upon you from the crown of your head to the soles of your feet.

You have spent your last ordinary moment.

I command your perception of the world to be seen through the focus of the blood of the cross of Christ.

I mark you now by that cross. Even as our Savior bears those marks, so you are changed this moment. Changed, to bear God's mark.

I mark you with the anointing of God. You will see as God sees and hear as God hears.

You will receive an insatiable hunger and desire for the courts of your God, and none of the pablum of this earth will satisfy your craving — for you are hungry and thirsty for your God.

I create within you a chasm that can only be filled by the flooding presence of the Holy Ghost.

Hunger for Him.

Thirst for Him.

Fight under Him and crown Him Lord of all.

Now, I bless you.

I release you from the fear of your past, the fear of your present, and the fear of your future.

I release you into the very bosom of the God who created this world and stuck a cross in the middle of it and hung His Son on it for your deliverance. May you know Him as no person has ever known Him, and may everywhere you go the tongued witness of the people declare, "The people of God are among us."

Now it is time to press forward, forgetting those things which are behind.

May this be your prayer: "**I press toward the mark for the prize of the high calling of God in Christ Jesus**" (Phil. 3:14).

Amen.

About the Author

Rod Parsley began his ministry as an energetic 19 year old, in the back yard of his parent's Ohio home. The fresh, "old–time gospel" approach of Parsley's delivery immediately attracted a hungry, God–seeking audience. From the 17 people who attended that first 1976 back yard meeting, the crowds grew rapidly.

Today, as the pastor of Columbus, Ohio's, 5200–seat World Harvest Church, Parsley oversees World Harvest's K–12 Christian Academy; World Harvest Bible Institute; and numerous church–sponsored outreaches, including Lifeline, a pro–life organization, Lightline, an anti–pornography league, and Breakthrough, World Harvest Church's daily and weekly television broadcast, currently heard by a potential audience of over 160 million people.

Rod Parsley also serves as Dr. Lester Sumrall's personal assistant in directing the End–Time Joseph "Feed The Hungry" program.

To contact the author
write:
Rod Parsley
World Harvest Church
P.O. Box 32932
Columbus, Ohio 43232

*Please include your prayer requests
and comments when you write.*

Books by Rod Parsley

Repairers of the Breach

The Backside of Calvary

God's Answer to Insufficient Funds

Tribulation to Triumph

**Available from your local bookstore
or from:**

HARRISON HOUSE
P. O. Box 35035
Tulsa, OK 74153

In Canada contact:

Word Alive
P. O. Box 284
Niverville, Manitoba
CANADA ROA 1EO

The Harrison House Vision

Proclaiming the truth and the power
Of the Gospel of Jesus Christ
With excellence;

Challenging Christians to
Live victoriously,